Water in the Wilderness

Francis W. Vanderwall, S.J.

Water in the Wilderness

Paths of Prayer,
Springs for Life

Paulist Press 🕊 *New York/Mahwah*

Library of Congress
Catalog Card Number: 84-62154

ISBN: 0-8091-2680-X

Published by Paulist Press
997 Macarthur Boulevard
Mahwah, New Jersey 07430

Printed and bound in the
United States of America

Contents

for the greater glory of God

*"The glory of God
is the person fully alive" (St. Irenaeus)*

With Gratitude

No book is written entirely alone. This one is no exception. I have been helped by many friends in its composition. They have taught me, they have challenged me, they have supported and encouraged me along the way. I am deeply grateful to each one of them.

I thank especially Jean Vanier and Janice Risse, Dianne Heindrich, C.D.P. and Tom Clancy, S.J., Kathy and Tom Rucker, and Paul Sheldon. Their criticisms of the first draft fashioned this book into what it is today. I also thank Rosemary McKay who generously typed the first draft, and Mary Giles Peresich, R.S.M. who meticulously brought the book to its final typed conclusion.

However, I take full responsibility for its content and any errors that may be in it, and in no way intend to pass on my failures to anyone else.

Behold, I am doing a new thing;
   now it springs forth, do you not perceive it?
I will make a way in the wilderness
   and rivers in the desert.
The wild beasts will honor me,
   the jackals and the ostriches;
For I give water in the wilderness,
   rivers in the desert,
To give drink to my chosen people,
   the people whom I formed for myself
That they might declare my praise.

(Is 43:19–21)

Introduction

Central to our Judaeo-Christian heritage of spirituality is the belief that God is not a distant entity but rather a personal Savior. We believe that in Jesus God has become enfleshed once and for all, making visible the previously invisible God. Through this faith we have been called to a radically new perception of ourselves and the entire universe around us. We have been challenged to believe that we are a people of immense worth and goodness, dearly loved by our Creator who sees us as nothing less than his own daughters and sons.

Yet the full impact of this amazing declaration of love frequently escapes us. We may profess faith in Jesus as the Incarnate Word of God but find it difficult to allow our lives to be transformed by that faith. We let it remain abstract and impersonal and don't quite know how to follow through with the natural consequences of our faith. Consequently we often find ourselves distant from the very faith that we profess and tend to look upon it as mostly irrelevant to the realities of daily living. And the daily living grinds on: the trials and disappointments, the betrayals and losses, the momentary occasions of festivity and joy that sometimes serve only to highlight the lack of a consistent hope in our lives. And we find ourselves in a desert parched and barren, with little relief in sight, and we may well ask the often unspoken question: Is this all there is to life? Is happiness so illusive that it appears to be more like a mirage than a reality? Often this question leads to religious questions. And we may ask: "Where is the God of love and compassion, the Incarnated God that is supposed to be immersed in our lives? When I most need him he is never around. I wonder whether there is any truth to him. Or is it a collection of teachings designed to keep me subservient to a Church that often resembles a secular institution rather than a spiritual one?" The doubts can then flow in several directions depending on the personality and the situation of the questioner. And the wilderness of life can appear so vast and desolate that the hope of ever finding water in it fades, leading to a sense of futility and hopelessness. Or it can lead to a rejection of the enfleshed God and all he represents with a resolute assertion of my own independence. A choice is made to forge ahead alone, expecting no help but rather trusting in my own prowess to make it through the wilderness and discover on my own the water that must be there, somewhere.

It is to counteract this all too frequently made choice that I write this book. I write it for all those good people who feel isolated and alone, who experience rejection and abandonment, who have trusted in God and feel let down by him, who have lost hope, or who are losing hope in ever finding the water that God has promised us in the wilderness of our lives. To some extent I think these people are all of us. Somewhere along the way we have felt the futility of faith and have wondered where the God of faith and all consolation dwells. We have wondered whether we are traveling the right road and speculate as to whether we will ever arrive at our destination.

This is because we have misplaced the road map and have forgotten the directions God has given us in Jesus.

We have been journeying for so long, have struggled to believe in the quest for so many years, that the words of the Teacher are remembered but vaguely. It is to refresh our memories that I write. For Jesus has told us, with an eagerness in his voice and no doubt a twinkle in his eye:

> The Kingdom of God is in your midst.
> Rejoice and let it shine forth.

Stop traveling. You have arrived. No need to journey any further. The water you have been looking for is here; open your eyes and see. Quench your thirst; the water is free for it is the water of life, it is the oasis of limitless freedom, and justice, and love.

But how does one open one's eyes? How does one recognize the truth that dwells in our midst? It can be very easy if one wants it; it is as easy as waking up after a long sleep. But waking up after a long sleep can take time. It is a process during which one gradually focuses in on the objects in the room and gently allows one's memories and thoughts to return to consciousness.

In the life of faith this process is what is called prayer. It is an awakening to the realization that we are not alone, to the recognition that we are dearly loved and have a tender, caring, compassionate companion in Jesus our Lord. It is the attentive listening to the whispers of love that can be heard from the depths of our very own being, reassuring us of our own intrinsic worth. It is the understanding of what it means to have within ourselves the fountain of living water, ever bubbling up fresh and sparkling, to refresh us and renew us with its life-giving properties.

This process of prayer is the process by which we rediscover what it means for us to be human. It is always done in companionship, never alone; it is companionship that affirms us as human. And through this companionship with the Lord of my heart, I begin to discover my own potential, my own lovableness and amazing uniqueness. It is the process of a love relationship. For just like the lover who enables his beloved to feel warmly cherished, so our Lord yearns to affirm us and enable us to feel the warmth of his love. And it is in experiencing this warmth that we come alive and allow our inner beauty to shine forth. It is this warmth of love that confirms our personal worth.

Discovering this inner beauty in the presence of a true lover enables us to rejoice in being human. But what is it that we have to celebrate? What does it mean for us to be human? It is an ontological question that touches the very core of the meaning of our existence. Until we can glimpse an answer we may have difficulty dealing with it. And it is precisely at this point that the process of prayer offers us the answer. For prayer is exercising one of our most uniquely human qualities, the ability we possess of being able to reflect on ourselves, to enter into a dialogue with our inner voice—the Voice that our faith tells us is nothing less than the Voice of our enfleshed God—and through this dialogue arrive at an understanding and appreciation of our own uniqueness and worth.

But this is only the beginning. As we use our abilities to reflect we begin to discover that to be human means that we are free. For as we experience the acceptance and affirmation of our indwelling God we begin to see that we do not have to prove ourselves to him. We see that no matter what we do he loves who we are and does not judge or condemn, but time and again gives us the safety of his all-forgiving embrace. And this is freedom indeed! However, there are many un-freedoms that can dominate and manipulate us. In prayer they begin to be seen as unnecessary obstacles to our happiness. We can be free; we can be truly the liberated human being that we so wish we could be.

For in this relationship of love we begin to discover what these obstacles are and we begin to discover how to break the bonds that shackle us. And in this we can celebrate being a human being, for is not freedom another fundamental characteristic of the human person?

But this is not all. As we recognize that we have the uniquely human ability to reflect and see, through the dialogue of prayer, that freedom is ours if we but want it, we also see that our greatest longing, the one that distinguishes us from the animals, is being satisfied. And that is the longing to love and to be loved. For love is the glory of the human being, the destiny and purpose of our existence, the magnificent triumph of our God made visible in and through his Son Jesus, and in and through each one of us. For it is in prayer that we meet the enfleshed God, and it is out of prayer that we develop the perspective of seeing that our God speaks to us in many ways, through many people. We can begin to appreciate what it means to have a God who is so involved with us that he gives us his only Son, by enfleshing him. From this we know that our God is in our world, immersed in it and in its affairs, and will forever be accessible to us if we reach out and let him.

This is the meaning of the incarnation. Our God, through his Son, Jesus, is intimately involved with our existence. He can hence be discovered not just in formal prayer but in the people around us, in the events of our day, in the history of our lives. He is found in the sciences and the arts, in our work and in our play, in all that we consider "secular" in our world. And the world itself becomes prayer. Hence meeting the enfleshed God in formal prayer is only the first step toward encountering his love in many other places. Often, we believe that God is to be found only in formal prayer or in church. This is an underdeveloped understanding of the incarnation. God can be found in the midst of all our activities and encountered, not in formal prayer alone. But this can only be appreciated if we are praying. Prayer is the key that unlocks not only our humanity but the Divinity that dwells amongst us. Since this is so it is important not to limit the places where our God can be found. Hence while formal prayer is important, it is not enough. It is but the initiatory point out of which our entire lives become prayer.

But for this initiatory point to become enfleshed we need to realize that while it is the beginning it is a far richer, a far more multi-faceted point of origin than many of us may believe it to be. Each one of us is different; each one of us has his or her own way of praying. The one that you find most appealing and satisfying for you is your way of praying. It is important not to "canonize" one particular way. If it appeals to you, use it, if it doesn't, use another.

I have tried to aid you in this search through this book. I have described briefly several methods of prayer. You may wish to try them in order, or just skip around, trying one that you are particularly drawn to one day, and if you find it unappealing in actual practice move to another, till you find one that suits you. Once you have found one that you enjoy, stick with it till the enjoyment wanes and then move on to another. Be flexible with yourself, and avoid the temptation of feeling locked into a particular method. It is the result that matters, not the way to it.

As various as are the methods of prayer, so also are the results. As one awakens to the exciting realization of how intertwined is our God with us and our lives, our very lives start taking on a new perspective. We begin to put on the mind of Jesus and view our lives not from our limited perspective but from his. And out of this "conversion" we can perceive anew and delight in the meaning of Jesus' saying: "The Kingdom of God is in your midst; rejoice and let it shine forth."

For we will experience a new freedom that wells up from within us shattering the bonds that shackle us; we will become attuned to justice and recognize injustice where it prevails with a greater acumen; we will be able to love with that astonishing abandon with which God loves us. We will be able to relish the ultimate implications of what it means to have a God who is Father, a Son of God who is Brother. To aid you in this I have tried to describe some of the consequences of prayer and the implications of these consequences in our lives. It is by no means an adequate description but rather one that points to many other descriptions that you will be able to understand on a personal level as you live out your own lives of prayer. I pray that as you understand you will enjoy, and that as you enjoy you will give thanks to the Lord who has so wonderfully entered into the very fabric of our existence.

1

Preparing To Pray

We live in a busy world. Our days are all too often a
series of activities, many essential for our livelihood and
sustenance, many quite unnecessary and extraneous. In
the midst of all our activity there are times when we may
long for some peace and quiet, yet somehow such times
appear elusive and unattainable. But does this have to be
the case? I know of many busy people who have recognized that unless they find some time in their day for solitude their entire day misses something qualitative about
it. There seems to be a depth lacking in all they do, and
even though they may do much, they feel a sense of dissatisfaction within themselves. Then, and this can happen
either in a moment of insight or over a period of time, they
realize that what is missing is time for themselves. This
recognition is the first step toward a process that if
embarked on can promise an entirely new perspective to
their lives. A new depth of meaning becomes possible,
and, quite literally, the quality of their existence can be
transformed by injecting it with an inner power and hope
that they just had not experienced before.

This missing ingredient—finding time for oneself—
has been experienced variously as solitude, meditation,
prayer, and the like. But whatever the form it is experi-

enced in, the need for it is becoming ever more critical in the busy marketplace of our working day. For solitude gives one space for oneself. And in this, reflection becomes possible. Hence solitude can make one more human, for in solitude the fruits of reflection can mature. It enables us to reflect on ourselves and discover there immense resources that we never knew existed. Solitude provides awareness and a greater understanding of ourselves, and, through that, of the people around us. This evokes a sensitivity and empathy that makes possible all that is most human about us to be discovered. Out of this discovery we come to realize that we are not alone, that within us is a voice that supports, encourages and affirms all our endeavors, and more importantly affirms ourselves, just as we are.

What is this voice? I call this voice God. It seems that Christians have not taken seriously enough the incarnation of God in his Son Jesus. It seems that we have allowed institutionalized religion, laws and commands to distance God from our lives. We tend to compartmentalize the God dimension in our lives and isolate it to a Sunday service or a Saturday Eucharist. We seem to think of God only in times of need, or when we recall his judgment, and fear for our eternal destiny. Yet the central act of Christian redemption speaks with great clarity of a God who is love, and who, through his Son Jesus, has for all time revealed God's plan of salvation to all of humankind. The entire redemptive act is one of an outpouring of Divine love for his people. It is a tender, compassionate, indescribably caring love. In it is not to be found judgment and condemnation but mercy and forgiveness. "God sent his Son into the world, not to condemn the world, but so that through him the world might be saved" (Jn 3:17). As Jesus says, the judgment and condemnation is for those who choose it by refusing to believe the power of God's Holy Spirit to forgive and heal. It is time we started taking

God's yearning to be truly a Father for us more seriously, and relinquish our uncertainties and fears of him. He is not an ogre. Maybe we tend to make him out to be one so that we can excuse ourselves for remaining as we are and consequently not have to deal with the radical transformation that encountering a God of true compassion and love can effect in us. Understandably. No one really wants change. The very word can sound negative, but if it can be viewed not as a painful process that can uproot the rhythms of our lives but as a process of healing, we may perhaps find it a bit more palatable. And if we can see it as an exciting opportunity to meet our amazing God, the healer of immense love, we may find that the changes flow naturally even as our wounds heal naturally when a physician prescribes a medication that merely increases the natural healing powers that our bodies contain. Experiencing God's love for us can effectively transform us into that person of peace and joy, love and freedom that we so long for. And yet we persist in doubting. This is such a terrible shame. God is anything but a demanding taskmaster or vindictive judge. He is anything but a distant being too remote for human discourse. He is a God who is passionately fond of his people and who has given humankind the greatest sign of his love by sending his Son, his only Son, Jesus, into our midst to become one of us, and by so doing to forever dispel any doubts we may have of his remoteness and unavailability. And yet are these doubts dispelled?

I think that the doubts prevail only when one does not take time to listen to oneself in solitude. If one allows solitude into one's life, the incarnation of God in Jesus can become a startling reality that can forever change the perspective of one's existence. Encountering God within oneself makes possible encounter with one's own humanity, for in that encounter we meet the very human God-man, Jesus. And we recognize that we are treasured by

11

him as precious earthen vessels regarded as immensely valuable and greatly loved, unique in all of creation.

Many of us may long for this encounter, but frequently do not know how to engage in it. We can agree that solitude, the chance to spend some time in reflection, is a very valuable thing to do, but we may not know how to go about it. Fortunately there are many excellent contemporary works available that can help us. I will try to mention some of them as we go along, but essentially what I will try to do will be to make available some of the many avenues to our inner selves that are available. There is no one way to God better than another. They are all good. If you encounter the God within through one of them, stay with that method till you feel that it is losing its effectiveness; then feel free to move away from it to another.

A word about methods in general. It is important not to canonize the way; it is the result that is important. And the results are what determine your success. One may feel in touch with one's center and sense close, loving relationship with God, and yet be quite insensitive and self-centered in one's relationships with other people. If this is the case, no matter how much time one spends in solitude, or how centered one may feel, God's friendship is probably being pre-empted in favor of spiritual exhibitionism. For the interior encounter with God, once engaged in sincerely, is an encounter of love, and like any love union ought to transform the beloved. This means that the feelings of joy and peace, freedom and love that one may be experiencing in solitude become naturally deflected into one's personal world. Hence the way to test the authenticity of one's times of reflection and solitude is to ask oneself some questions: Do I have greater love for others? Am I more patient with them? Am I being less judgmental? Do I really love my enemies? Have I become humbler? Do I yearn more and more for the friendship of

Jesus? Am I less controlled by my desires for power and wealth? Am I accepting myself more just as I am? And so on. It is the answers to questions such as these that determine the authenticity of one's experiences in solitude. For all of this to happen there are some prerequisites though. They may initially appear self-evident but need to be highlighted at the outset for clarity's sake.

First, it is very necessary that one make a decision. Without a firm decision to set a time aside for solitude and reflection, the distractions of our daily activities will quickly lead us away from our resolve. One has to first say to oneself, "Yes, this is very important for me; I am going to do it."

Second, one has to find the time. I have found that many sincere people make the commitment but then don't pin themselves down to a specific time, and all too often this leads to neglect and eventual abandonment. A decision firmly made but not put into practice remains but a decision firmly made. Finding time now, as we all know, is not that easy. It is the first test of our resolve. I think it can be made a lot easier if we liberate ourselves from some pre-conceived notions that limit the places of our solitude.

And this is the third prerequisite. Finding a place may be easier than one thinks if one uses one's imagination and allows some flexibility in one's daily routine. Once I had a directee who was really getting frustrated about finding a good location for solitude. He tried everything, his home, an hour earlier or later in the office with the door closed, using his lunch break, but none of them worked. I asked him how long a drive he had to work and back. He said, "Oh, about half an hour." "Great," I said. "What do you do in your car during that time?" "Listen to the news," he replied. "Fine," I said. "How about turning off the radio and allow your car to become as it were your portable cell?" He looked at me uncertainly. "I don't know," he said, "but I'll try it." "O.K." I replied. "Here's what you do. Just take a quote from Scripture, one of your favorite passages for a start, or I can suggest some for you, and then, picking out the word or line that touched you the most as you first read it, reflect on it as you drive to work, listening to what you feel the while." "Fine," he replied. "I'll try it." He did, and after only a few short days he reported feeling a whole lot calmer, less frenetic at work, and much more attentive to his wife and children upon returning home. We can find our own portable cell to meet the Lord within, and in its finding our lives can begin to be transformed from within.

Finding a place for solitude calls for creativity at times, but once we allow ourselves to break away from the traditional places for prayer and begin to believe that God can really be found in any place, it may surprise us how easy it is to discover our own private place for communion with the God within. One's own room, a church, a city park, even an automobile can become that place out of which the inner resources and strengths that we possess can be discovered and nutured.

But how do we engage his Spirit dwelling within us? Presuming that we have located our "portable cell," how do we begin to allow the voice of God to be heard? This leads us to the fourth prerequisite. By listening to our hearts. The word "heart" perhaps needs to be clarified. It is one of those frequently used words that has lost much of its spiritual meaning through misuse and overuse in inappropriate places. The heart in the Hebrew tradition was not merely the seat of one's feelings. Feelings now are certainly important, but heart includes all that is within us that is non-corporeal. Hence it includes thoughts, reflections, hopes, desires, dreams, insights, and the affections with its whole array of feelings, moods and intangible sensations that are nevertheless very real, and emanate from within us. The heart then includes all that makes us uniquely human, that spiritual dimension in our lives that differentiates us essentially from machines. It is by paying attention to these various movements that we hear the voice of God speak to us with an eloquence that sometimes can be startling.

Central to this process is listening. Our world is cluttered with noises. All too often we may find ourselves involuntarily turning off the barrage of words that come at us from so many sources. But more often than not we seek the noise of words and allow them to inundate our senses, etherizing as it were our own feelings and thoughts in the process. We allow the radio, TV, the newspapers, the telephone, the highway billboards, our own friends and family to inflict upon us a barrage of words from the time we wake up in the morning till we retire for the night. Allowing this on a daily basis, week after week, month after month can effectively repress all that is most noble and spiritual about us, making us more robot-like than human.

In choosing solitude and electing for a listening heart we contradict this temptation and choose instead to reassert our deepest longings to become a happier human being again. But this, while many may find it desirable, is difficult to actually do. It is amazing the number of excuses, all legitimate of course, that I make for myself in order to avoid entering into solitude. Daily I have to discipline myself to choose it, and daily I can come up with a million other things I've got to do before settling down for my time alone with God and myself. It takes a discipline that ought to come from within. But we are not angels; it would perhaps be easier if we were but we are men and women susceptible to all the distractions of our race and our time. Hence, it would be most beneficial to initially set up a definite time in one's day for solitude, and then stick to it. The more it is adhered to the easier it becomes, because once one starts experiencing the riches to be discovered in this inward journey the desire for it develops more and more from within and the external constraints become correspondingly less imperative.

But how do we listen to our hearts? There are several ways, but I think the initial stage of active listening begins with learning to become still. Discipline is called for here since it is not that easy for us to sit still. It takes effort, and knowledge of how to go about it. We can, for instance, begin by closing our eyes and focus our thoughts and feelings on a single idea or word. I find repeating a short phrase such as a saying of Jesus very helpful. I may say, "Come to me, all you who labor and are overburdened and I will give you rest" (Mt 11:29-30), slowly and attentively, pausing at each phrase, or I may simply say the name of Jesus over and over in conjunction with my breathing. What this does is relax me and provide the focus I need for my solitude at the same time. Another method of slowing down and focusing oneself could arise from a simple exercise of concentrating on each part of my body, starting with my feet, and gradually moving up to my head, simply commanding the part concentrated on to become relaxed, or begin to feel like a stone or a piece of wood. For those who are aware of self-hypnosis and know of its value, it too can be a very effective way of not only becoming very still and focused but also of facilitating in a remarkable way a heightened state of consciousness that in turn enables listening to oneself.

These methods of becoming still can, in themselves, be prayer. There are many prejudices associated with the word "prayer." But, I think, if we can set aside for a while the limited understanding of prayer that most of us have, we can perhaps start to discover the array of riches true prayer can gift us with. Prayer has suffered from an unfair, inaccurate and bad reputation in the eyes of many. Often it is considered the activity of the naive, children, the elderly, priests and religious. It has been viewed as a "talking to God" type of activity that has little relevance to the real world and the real problems one has to face in it. It has also been seen as a futile activity, a talking to oneself, and a hoping that an infuriatingly silent God is around somewhere to hear us. This is most regrettable. Fortunately today more and more "busy executive types" are recognizing that the often quite infantile understandings of prayer that they have been taught are woefully inadequate descriptions of what true prayer can be.

What is prayer? It is a listening to the various movements going on within oneself—this means listening to one's "heart" in the full sense of that word—and believing that in those movements God himself is speaking to you. It means engaging in a dialogue with one's inner voice, believing that in that dialogue one is experiencing an encounter with God himself. It is important that it be truly a dialogue and not a monologue. This means that when one recites a phrase from Scripture or the name of Jesus or delights in a flower or savors the moods and events of the day, one pauses and listens to the response that that word or feeling or thought causes in one's heart. It is in that heartfelt response that God's voice is heard. When the feeling or thought is so aroused, entertain it, savor it, let it permeate your being, tasting its content with deliberateness, and relish it until the feeling wanes. For example, we can begin to pray by reviewing the events of our day. Take today, for instance, and prior to going to sleep tonight, or first thing in the morning if one is too tired, simply remember the various experiences of the day, both the significant ones as well as the insignificant. Do this not necessarily in chronological order but in order of importance. If, for example, you had a very pleasant luncheon engagement, begin there, or if you experienced some unpleasantness at work, use that experience as a starting point. This review now ought not to be done alone. The great advantage of believing in a God who yearns for intimacy with his people is that he is always available to console, to support and love, to share in one's joys and pleasant times. So, make a conscious effort to invite God into the marketplace of your day, and share with him the events of your day as you review them. This is much like sharing your day with your beloved over an evening meal, as opposed to keeping it inside yourself by dining alone. This is done by simply listening to your heart's response to a particular event or experience and then mentally share with him your feelings about it. Then engage in a dialogue with him about your feelings, asking him either for solace or guidance, or simply delighting with him over the gift of a pleasant luncheon or a difficult moment at work, for there is often a gift in a painful event. There are many other points from which prayer can begin, but the process involves essentially a listening to one's heart and responding from that point to what emanates from there. Listening to one's heart is, in a pragmatic sense, a "useless" undertaking. Compared to washing dishes, paying bills, going to work and earning money in one's chosen occupation, listening to one's heart appears as an out-of-kilter, non-relevant unnecessary type of thing to do. It is. One will accomplish nothing, one will look back on one's time of solitude and see that financially it was a bust. All one did was just sit there, take up space and attend to one's inner self. A waste of time! Or was it?

If one wants to relish life a little more, become capable of delighting in the richness of being a human being, appreciate with a greater intensity one's own lovableness and the love another has for you and become through this a greater lover, one can hardly forego this "useless" activity. For it is precisely by engaging in it that one taps the profound and varied resources one has, to become that vitally alive human being that one feels one can be. It is what can make one become that reflective person that can effectively transform one's outlook on life and put one in the driver's seat again. It begins by making a decision, then finding a time and a suitable place, followed by the attentive listening to one's heart, and finally responding to what is evoked there. The method, I must repeat, is not the point; the point is listening to oneself and the God within who is yearning to bring us myriad gifts that will transform the entire universe around us. If we enter into this discipline regularly, if not daily, we will be able to see the rainbow in the storm and from within ourselves will arise the strength and the power we need to not only deal with the rapid changes occurring in our world but indeed join them, changing them into forces for good and not evil, both for ourselves and for our neighbors far and near.

I have tried to introduce you to solitude in this section and allow that to lead into a brief reflection on prayer. I will now try to offer you a variety of ways to pray and hope that they will open up for you the vast riches that a lifetime of praying and solitude can give you. It is out of this practice that I believe we can begin to avoid compromising our very humanity to the dehumanizing elements of an automated world. Through it we can recognize that by reasserting our humanity we are really reaffirming our divinity in Christ who dwells within us. We can hear that he is inviting us always to choose greatness with him, for he has already chosen it for us by inviting us to become his own sisters and brothers. Not only that, but to become co-heirs with him in his Kingdom of peace and justice, of joy and abundant love, to be nothing less than daughters and sons of the living God who with a gentle yearning speaks so fondly to our hearts.

2

Varieties of Prayer

There are a variety of ways for developing our capacity for reflection in the context of solitude. I will try to outline and explain briefly some of them in this chapter. No one way is necessarily better than another. The way that attracts you and that works for you is your particular way. This, of course, will change. You may find it becoming boring or tedious after several days or weeks. If this occurs, change to another method that may attract you. You may feel that you are "putting in the time" but you are not becoming a more loving, sensitive person. If this occurs, talk to a spiritual director about your prayer, ask yourself whether you are open to the consequences of prayer, and the like. For a concrete way of determining whether you are succeeding in your prayer life is to monitor the rest of your life. Are you becoming more alive to the world you live in, more aware of injustice in its various forms? Are you experiencing a greater freedom within yourself, an increasing sensitivity to the poor and the oppressed?

For prayer is not something I do for myself alone; it is for the good of my brothers and sisters as well. In this sense, when I am in solitude I am not alone, for in this place of quiet reflection I begin to realize that I am a part of a community of believers, brothers and sisters throughout the world, all praying to our one Father who eagerly wants to give us all good things if we but ask him. This means that I become aware not only of how much I am valued and treasured by God but how much God values and treasures my brothers and sisters. And in turn this awareness ought to lead me to valuing and treasuring my brothers and sisters with that quality of love with which God has loved me. A sign of a successful prayer life then is to be found not in the solitude out of which it begins but in the marketplace of our daily lives where we live out, in a natural outpouring of love, the care and the self-sacrifice, the peace and the joy, the justice and the forgiveness for our brothers and sisters that our personal experience of God has enabled us to encounter in our own lives. This is why a life of prayer ought to transform not only ourselves but the entire world.

I will now offer you some of the many ways of getting the most benefit from your time of solitude. I will try to describe each of them and hopefully make them as non-technical as possible. They are not in any particular order, for they are merely ways, not the end. The end is for you to discover as you utilize these means.

Awareness

One of the great stumbling blocks to prayer for the contemporary human person is that one feels one has to *do* it. Often I find a retreatant entering a retreat eager and ready to get on with it. There is a desire to "get the job done" in all of us. Our modern world has equated human worth with accomplishments to such an extent that one brings this mentality to prayer. Understandably. There is the feeling that if *I* am not praying, if *I* am not accomplishing prayers, covering territory as it were, *I* am really not praying. The emphasis is more on me doing something rather than me doing nothing. Doing nothing, after all, is non-productive, and if I'm not producing I am not really praying, and hence I am not a very good person, perhaps even a hypocrite, pretending to pray and really not praying, and so the reasoning goes!

When a person enters prayer with such a mentality— and that seems to be the case for most of us—I suggest that he or she *not* pray. This is usually met with initial incredulity. "What do you mean, not pray?" is the sometimes spoken question. After all that is what I am to do here, is it not? "Well, yes," I reply, "but praying is really not *me* doing it but rather God doing it in me. The action is his, not mine and what we do is try to let him. So," I continue, "forget about praying and simply begin to relax and let things be."

The "letting things be" is, of course, easier said than done. We are not oriented toward simply be-ing. We are accomplishers, do-ers, not be-ers. This is where I find an awareness exercise very helpful.

Again, like the Jesus Prayer, it is deceptively simple. It consists of becoming still by concentrating on oneself. Sounds selfish. But its consequences are very selfless. What it enables is an inward tranquility that, quite apart from being selfish, makes it possible for one to forget oneself. And as this happens one is in the presence of the God within, being with him, and allowing him to be with us, with little or no distraction. It makes possible a profound stillness and in that stillness makes possible the presence of God to be sensed. It is not that God is sensed out of the stillness but rather that in the stillness itself God becomes experienced.

How does one go about practicing awareness? First, I think, by setting aside our traditional prejudices about what prayer ought to be. Don't even call it prayer. It's just an exercise to help one become more aware of oneself. Then, become very still. Now, begin to concentrate on

22

your body. Simply become aware of the various pressure points, starting wherever you like. Let us say you begin with your back. Merely concentrate on the pressure of your back against the chair. Sense the pressure of your back pressing against the chair. Avoid any analysis or intellectual reasonings. Just become conscious of your back against the chair. Now, slowly move to your shoulders, and the gentler pressure of your clothing on them. Take your time about it. Then you may want to move on down your arms doing the same thing. Become aware of the gentle pressure of the air about your arms, and simply rest in that awareness. Then feel the air playing between your fingers. Do likewise with them.

Move through your whole body sensing the various pressures, some slight, others more intense, all the way down to your feet pressing against your shoes. Rest in the awareness of these pressures. And don't forget to concentrate on the pressures about your face and the crown of your head. There are pressures there too! In fact, there is not a part of our bodies that is devoid of pressure. It is just that we are not conscious of it. Become conscious, slowly, deliberately, and an amazing stillness will overcome you.

And that's it! Where is God in this? I repeat, in the stillness, in the quiet tranquility that this exercise generates. Simply stay in this state, moving from one pressure point to another, and you will be in his presence. No words, no profound thought, no brilliant insights, just a simple resting in God, even as a little child would rest contentedly in the arms of his father or mother. Very much like the invitation of the psalmist who is not concerned with "lofty ambitions" or "great affairs," "marvels beyond my scope," but rather notes that it is:

Enough for me to keep my soul tranquil and quiet
  like a child in its mother's arms,
As content as a child that has been weaned (Ps 131:2).

If one practices awareness on a daily or regular basis, one can soon begin to experience a ripple effect in one's day. Things will just not overwhelm you as much; the harsher events, the apparently insoluble difficulties, the frustrations of standing in lines take on a less threatening stance, for you now walk with heightened consciousness, aware of an inner power and strength that you were perhaps not as aware of before. And in that awareness you allow your human vitality to become ever more activated and operative.

For practicing awareness in prayer in various forms and developing what I have written here for you, I strongly recommend *Sadhana: A Way to God* by Anthony de Mello, S. J. (Institute for Jesuit Sources, Fusz Memorial, St. Louis University, 3700 West Pine Blvd., St. Louis, Mo. 63108).

The Jesus Prayer

Jesus is the Son of God. He entered this world not to condemn it but to save it for an eternal life of indescribable joy. Any person who chooses to be, or to remain, Christian, therefore, is one who professes belief in Jesus as the Savior of the world. Christians, furthermore, believe that this Jesus has made the inaccessible God of power and might accessible to anyone who calls on his name. The Christian believes that in Jesus we have the key to unlock all that is most mysterious about God, and in that unlocking to discover what is most mysterious about ourselves. If one goes to Jesus, the perfect man because he is God, we can discover all that we can be as we strive for our own perfection as human beings. For the perfect human being is Divinity exposed in each one of us.

Out of these beliefs there developed in the third and fourth centuries A.D. in the sands of the Egyptian desert a spirituality both simple and profound. It was a spirituality that had at its core a belief in Jesus as Savior and Lord. It began out of a single-minded desire to follow Christ alone by leading a life of radical solitude and prayer, and through it to arrive at a union with God that was believed to be unattainable in the midst of the distractions of an urban area. The desert was viewed as the appropriate place for this union not only because it was isolated from the world, but also because it was believed to be the domain of demons. Doing battle with demons was seen as an essential part of getting close to God, for it was believed that God was most intimately present to them in the midst of the battle. Calling out to God for help brought him into their midst with an intimacy that would otherwise be difficult to experience.

Their lives itself dictated their prayer. They were lives characterized by simplicity, common sense and love. Their prayers were the psalms recited in order throughout the week, interspersed with what has come to be known as the Jesus Prayer.

The Jesus Prayer in its entirety is as follows:

Lord Jesus Christ, Son of God, have mercy on me, a sinner.

It is a short sentence, but if repeated with reverence and attention it is capable of producing an inner quiet and calm that in a very short time can still oneself and place oneself in the presence of God—which was the lifetime goal of these good men and women of the desert.

For one wishing to enter into a life of quiet listening to God within, I find this Jesus Prayer an excellent place to begin. What happens is that as one engages the mind, in the utterance of the words, one gradually allows the words to sink into one's heart as it were, and then the words cease being an intellectual thing and become an immediate experience of God's presence to the pray-er.

It's as if in the very uttering of the words communication with God takes place and one begins to feel, from one's own center, the forgiveness, the mercy and the love flowing outward to permeate one's entire being.

As the practice of this prayer develops one may reduce even the short phrase to the single word "Jesus."

Jesus, as our Savior, is all we need for our complete wholeness as a human being. No matter the anxieties and trials that may beset us, calling on his name in faith can bring a remarkable calming and a confidence that will well up from one's very center. It is a very effective way of reaching out to God, and finding him within, waiting, eager to reach out and to bring healing to his wounded daughter or son.

It is important to avoid skepticism as to the effectiveness of the Jesus Prayer because of its simplicity. It is also important to believe that by calling on the name of Jesus in faith he will answer, and that that answer will rise up from within oneself in an almost immediate calming, a sense of developing confidence that our God is indeed alive and living within us. I said "immediate." Initially it may take a little longer, not because of the inefficiency of the prayer itself but because it may take the beginning pray-er a little time to get into its apparently simple rhythm.

I find that one way of "getting into it" that has proved effective is to coordinate the saying of each phrase in the sentence with one's breathing. So, as one breathes in, one says, "Jesus," and then as one breathes out, one says, "Son of God" and so on. It is not necessary to say a phrase with every breath. Rather, as you recite the phrase with your breathing in and out, savor it for a few breaths or longer, before moving on to the next phrase.

Another way of "getting into" the Jesus Prayer is to simply take the name of Jesus alone. Breathe the name of Jesus into yourself, and then, as you breathe out, name an anxiety that may be uppermost on your mind as you came to prayer and sense it flowing out of you. I think naming the anxiety is very helpful, for naming it focuses it, and that enables the healing to occur with a greater facility. So, breathe Jesus in, breathe out an anxiety and then rest in the feelings of peace and harmony you may sense there. If you don't immediately sense this peace, simply repeat the prayer over and over again until eventually you do. Sometimes it is hard to sense Jesus' presence within us because of the usual distractions that accompany prayer. But persistence and a sharpening focus on what one is doing usually stills the mind, so much so that one becomes completely taken up with Jesus entering into one's inner being. This intensifies with the ensuing release as one breathes out one's uppermost and named anxiety, providing a tangible confirmation, as it were, of Jesus' healing presence within. This can leave the pray-er in a state of delightful relaxation and gratitude, for what one is experiencing is the healing power of Jesus in one's life. As one engages in this process, in fact, one may find it unnecessary to actually say the name "Jesus," for now one can just sense him entering in with every breath, and one likewise can sense the releasing of the anxiety as one exhales.

What this prayer leads to is to the first step in fulfilling the injunction of St. Paul to "pray always." Frequent times of solitude with the Jesus Prayer can very soon overflow into your daily activities, so much so that no matter what you are doing you are delightfully aware of the presence of Jesus within, directing, consoling and loving you throughout your day.

The consequences of practicing this prayer are many, and each pray-er will discover for himself or herself the specific benefits of it. But, in general, it enables an intimacy to develop between Jesus and the individual that breeds a confidence. This, in turn, leads to a stance toward life that becomes gradually more and more positive, for one now knows, not just intellectually through the eyes of faith, but experientially, that one is not alone. And in that heartfelt knowledge one feels capable of not only facing but triumphing over the forces in one's day that appear threatening and inimical to one's existence.

For further reading on the Jesus Prayer I highly recommend *The Way of a Pilgrim* (Doubleday, Image Books) and *The Jesus Prayer for Today* by Arthur A. Vogel (Paulist Press, N.Y.). They will flesh out the skeletal outline of the Jesus Prayer that I have offered you here.

The Prayer of All Things

Come, let us walk into a garden. It is almost dusk; the sun is a huge ball of fiery orange as it descends into the earth. The birds are singing their evensong; the crickets are beginning their nightly chorus.

We walk slowly, very slowly, down the garden path covered with magnificent trees of all types. Green moss grows on some branches; on others there are vines with flowers blooming. There are also low blooming shrubs, some well manicured, others growing wild. They give off a scent that excites the senses. The white flowers on them contrast with the dark green of the shrub leaves.

Further down the path we come across tall-sentinelled pine trees, and their towering majesty compels us to look skyward where myriad shades of color greet us as the sun leaves behind it variegated remnants of its light filtered through the atmosphere. We pause and take in the beauty, and even as we watch the colors are changing, into darker mauves and richer oranges.

The path winds on and now we begin to become aware of the activity around us. Squirrels are scurrying here and there, one now chasing another, pausing, extending a quizzical look in our direction and then registering a little vocal protest before flying into the air onto the branch of another tree, further away from us.

We listen to the birds continue their evensong and watch them as they dart here and there, pausing to chirp merrily, or to sing invitingly to a nearby mate. They are like little darts of color, unpredictably flying off in various directions prior to their eventual resting for the night.

The path continues on and now emerges out of the woods into a little field rich for the harvest. Golden stalks of grain are billowing gently in the breeze, reflecting the dying rays of light as they do. We walk up to them and touch them, grains that will provide food for life. We bend down and scoop up some soil, and feel it slowly in our hands—the good earth. We let it fall back to the ground.

And then an unexpected but pleasant surprise. A rabbit, busily nibbling, keeps a watchful eye on us. We watch it for a while and then stroll on. Startled by our movement the rabbit darts away into the underbrush.

On our return we sense the cool breeze of evening brushing gently against our faces, and delight in it. The forested path is much darker now and the trees take on almost human shape as they protect us with their over-hanging presence. We walk up to one, and touch the trunk of a towering giant. It feels rough and sturdy, stolid in its firm rootedness, evidently a veteran of many storms that unsuccessfully attempted to uproot it.

We return from our walk, different, somehow calmer, somehow aware of an immense treasure experienced. There is a sense of richness, of belonging to something far bigger than ourselves and yet integrally part of ourselves. And from within we sense a peace and a contentment, an awareness that we have just seen, in a tangible way, the presence of God in our midst. And we quietly whisper a thanks.

This is the prayer of all things. It is very simple, a delight to do, and is the ideal prayer for one who has had a harried day at work, or one who has felt that the forces of the world were all converging upon him or her at one time. The prayer of all things gives perspective, it brings tranquility and calmness, and out of that calm it can eloquently speak of a God abundant in his generous gift-giving. Becoming conscious of this, savoring it, and luxuriating in it brings a sense of union, of belonging to One who is yearning to share his gifts with us if we let him.

It is important, when praying in this way, to allow yourself to truly pause and absorb the beauty around you. And it is better to attend to particular things than just the general beauty. Allow yourself to be absorbed by the beauty of a flower, just one flower, and let your feelings emerge from within, not in a mechanical sort of way, but naturally. Simply let the wonder of the flower speak to your heart, and when your heart responds, let it.

Your gratitude can be essentially unvoiced here; it can be more a feeling response of delight or praise or happiness; but let it be a natural thing. If you feel compelled to express your thanks verbally, keep it simple. A short thank you suffices. Simplicity ought to be the mood and humility the consequence. If one truly absorbs the magnificence of a tree, a single tree, the mood of simplicity and the attitude of humility ought to be a natural consequence.

The prayer of all things can truly be a delightful experience. It is so easy to do and yet it can produce a calmness within and an awareness of God's love for you in a most intimate way. It can affirm your own worth and immense value profoundly, and out of that affirmation you can discover resources within you that will enable you to face confidently a world that may belittle your own worth as a human person.

In summary, the prayer of all things then can be done as follows: (1) Go for a slow—the slower the better—walk through a garden. The more isolated the better at the beginning, though later you could do it anywhere—even at home, absorbing the beauty of your house plants, or the fish in your fish tank. (2) Allow yourself to pause over a leaf or a flower, a bird or a squirrel, whatever, and delight in the gift if offers you of beauty, and life, and miracle. (3) Stay with whatever feelings may well up from within you, and relish them for as long as they are present. Then move on to some other gift of nature and do the same. (4) If as you are delighting in the gifts you feel the need to articulate your praise, a thanks to the God-within, do so simply and humbly. I heard somewhere that when one truly appreciates a tree, let us say, that tree becomes your own tree, it becomes your own gift no matter where it is planted. Through appreciating the many gifts in nature it won't be long before you could be gifted with a garden complete with flowers, birds, squirrels, and even a few rabbits just for you to enjoy and savor.

To help you enter into this prayer I recommend *Prayer for All Times* by Pierre Charles, S.J. (Christian Classics: Westminster, Md., 1964). It is a book that for years I have found most enriching and helpful. I pray that you too will find in it treasures for your heart.

Praying with Music

One of the many benefits we have received as a consequence of Vatican Council II is the liturgical renewal. The updating of the liturgy has opened the way for the composition of many fine contemporary songs of prayer, most based entirely on Sacred Scripture. They provide us with a prayer form that is not only musically enriching but also is an avenue of accessibility to Scripture passages that may otherwise have been unavailable to us. Further, thanks to the wonder of modern electronic reproduction we can benefit from them through either records or tapes that enable us to hear them, listen to them with our hearts, and pray over them in the privacy of our own "hermitage." No longer are we restricted to hearing God's word in church or temple but rather, in a most palatable way, it can easily enter the most private place of our solitude.

Praying with music has its dangers. I think that for a start, if one chooses to use this form of prayer, it would be better to restrict oneself to liturgical music, preferably music based on Sacred Scripture. It would also be helpful to use music that one is familiar with through either having listened to it in a public worship context or having heard it previously somewhere else. This is because if one were to listen to new music in the context of one's prayer the possibility of being distracted by the music itself is present, precluding, consequently, the savoring of the heartfelt response to it. Also, I think it better to confine oneself just to liturgical music for a start, since it is more specifically music for prayer than, let us say, symphonic music would be. This is not to preclude symphonic music but rather to caution the pray-er of the dangers inherent in it. Symphonic music plumbs various emotions and frequently changes from one mood to another, from an adagio to a presto, and the like. These sometimes dramatic changes can disrupt one's mood of recollection, and quite apart from helping one pray, they could easily distract one away from prayer. I think that if one does choose to use classical music it would be better to go back to renaissance music, a music that is relatively repetitive in its musical statements. For example, I have found Pachelbel's *Canon in D Major* helpful for prayer, or, in a more contemporary vein, Grieg's *Peer Gynt Suite's* morning music, and Vaugh-Williams' *The Lark Ascending.* Usually, though, I avoid classical music for prayer because I find myself listening more to the music than to my heart. Of course, listening intently to the music can be an excellent way of sensitizing yourself and opening yourself to the beauty in the music, but I feel that for prayer the feelings evoked by the music have to be taken a further step. And this is the mutual sharing of your feelings with the God-within through praising and thanking him for the music's genius, and seeing it as a gift for you from him. Hence if you do feel attracted to praying with classical music, it would be good to start with a piece familiar to you so that the music could be more of a backdrop to your prayer than the focus of attention.

How about using other types of music for prayer? I mean music such as that developed by pop stars and themes from movies and the like. While some claim to have been able to pray well with these, I have difficulty doing so. But that could be a personal bias and hence it ought not to be generalized. I think the norm here ought to be: If it brings you peace and a greater sensitivity to God's love, use it! It must be kept in mind, though, that the point is not listening to music but allowing the music to be the conduit through which one encounters the God-within and hence one's own core of authenticity.

Returning now to liturgical music, let me recommend some composers whom I feel offer the best music for prayers. The music of the St. Louis Jesuits, published by the North American Liturgy Resources, 10802 N. 23rd Ave., Phoenix, Arizona 85029, as well as the music of Carey Landry and the Dameans, also produced by the same company, is helpful. The Monks of the Weston Priory, the music of John Michael Talbot and the works of Lucien Diess likewise can provide excellent accessibility to the depths of one's being. I think it is worth noting that not all of the compositions are equally helpful; listen to them and decide for yourself what is most beneficial for you and then use those particular compositions for your prayer.

But how does one pray with liturgical music? Let me outline for you what I have found helpful: (1) Select the music you want to pray with, preferably staying with just one or two songs, and set them up either on your record player or tape machine. Use the equipment that takes least effort to turn on and off. (2) Then, using the usual techniques, still yourself and begin to calm down. (3) Put the music on and allow its melody and words to touch your heart. (4) Turn it off at the end of the song and listen to your feelings and thoughts, resting in them for as long as they are present. (5) When they abate, go on to the next song or repeat the same song, and so on. It is perhaps necessary to re-emphasize that the prayer begins in its most authentic form in the listening that occurs both with the music as well as after it ends. (6) Allow yourself to dialogue with God about whatever was evoked in you from the music, and rest in his responses to you, savoring them in your heart.

Praying with music can be an excellent way to pray if one is traveling. Many people in today's mobile society discover that they spend many hours driving around, either running errands, or, for some, such as salespeople, traveling as a part of one's job. For them this prayer form can be used, with some minor adaptations. Let us say you have a trip coming up today that will take some time. Take a cassette tape recorder, select your favorite liturgical music and take it with you in the car. Then, simply play it while driving and let the music itself speak to your heart. I have found that on long trips especially, praying with music has proven most beneficial. It also can make you very alert to all that is going on around you, especially the road, and can become a method of experiencing a oneness with the world passing you by that brings with it its own consolation. The results of using music to pray with while traveling are many. A boring drive can be transformed into a loving encounter with God, a sense of solidarity with the people you pass on the road can evoke in you feelings of compassion and love, and you can encounter the consoling presence of God within you on what otherwise could very well be a lonely drive. Convert your car into your portable cell and you may find that your car can instruct you in ways that you never expected!

Once a friend of mine had to make frequent trips of some hours' duration on a regular basis. He resented the time he had to spend driving and wished he could avoid the journey. I suggested to him one day that he try taking some liturgical tapes with him and play them when he felt bored. He did. Some months later I asked him how his trips were working out. "Great!" he said, "I took your advice and now find that I am actually looking forward to my trips, for they give me a unique opportunity to be alone with God, just the two of us with no chance of interruptions on the way. Also," he went on, "the trips seem to be getting much shorter!"

It is an adaptation to the mobile world we live in that once again can facilitate an experience of God that can leave us not resentful but grateful for the opportunity of being alone with ourselves, and with the God dwelling within.

Meditation on Sacred Scripture

Meditation is one of those much-used words that frequently has as many meanings as there are people using it and hearing it. It is an umbrella word that covers a variety of ways for reaching into oneself and there encountering the God-within. There is some validity in most of the techniques it encompasses. I am using it here in one limited sense of the word, namely, meditation on Sacred Scripture or some other sacred work that contains in its words a power that charges them with an ability to go beyond the words themselves.

It is a way of meeting the God-within through the doorway of one's mind. It is a process that asks the prayer to reflect on a passage of Scripture, let us say, and then listen to what one feels as a consequence of that reflection. It engages one's "heart" in its various capacities, beginning with the intellectual apprehension of the words, then the quiet reflecting on the words, and finally a relishing of the feelings aroused by them. It can be a source of great insight and comfort. It can also challenge and console, invite and strengthen the pray-er.

In this description I am confining myself to Sacred Scripture. This is because I am most familiar with it as a source for meditation and because I have found it to be one of the best gateways to discovering truth in myself.

First, a word about Sacred Scripture. Scripture is not just another book. For centuries its words have transformed lives, and indeed entire movements. I am reminded of Abba Anthony, the acknowledged father of monasticism. One day in church he heard the words of Jesus "Be perfect as your heavenly Father is perfect," and immediately they triggered within him a desire to respond to that invitation. His response not only transformed his own life but served as a model for hundreds of other people to follow his example and leave all they had to go into the desert and there seek the salvation promised them. Monasticism as we know it today evolved out of this, and the rich spiritual heritage it offers us gives ample testimony to the power of the words in Sacred Scripture.

But how does one go about meditating on Sacred Scripture? I think the first prerequisite is to make sure one has a good, up-to-date Bible that has the latest results of biblical scholarship. We are living in an exciting time for biblical scholarship. The discovery of the Qumran Scrolls greatly increased the developing impetus for accurate translations of the Bible. Recent research in the allied fields of history, archeology and literary criticism has further enabled us today to have Bibles that are far more faithful to the original Hebrew and Greek than the sixteenth century English translations that had been our only access to the Word of God. We need to capitalize on this and make sure we have a Bible that has the latest scholarship so that the Word of God can be revealed to us with a greater clarity and accurateness.

Once one has chosen a Bible faithful to the original text, familiarizing oneself with it could begin. This ought not to be engaged in as a study primarily, though that certainly would be beneficial, but rather one should page through it, getting used to it, becoming accustomed to its format. Many people have favorite "Bible stories" or passages. Rereading them and locating them in their context could further enhance one's familiarity with the books of the Bible as a whole. It may help to remember that what is referred to commonly as the Bible is really a library of books, several texts therefore, each written in its own style and set in its own historical context. Familiarizing oneself with all of this can be an engaging and rewarding task in itself. It is important not to feel that one has to be very familiar with the Bible in order to pray with it, however, for that familiarity can be long in coming and is really not necessary for prayer.

In order to pray, begin by picking out a few favorite passages, or if you have no favorites, simply begin by taking the readings from the upcoming Sunday's liturgy, and start there. Or you may wish to talk to someone versed in the Bible, a teacher, a priest or deacon, a rabbi or a religious, for example, who could guide you in choosing passages from Scripture that may be beneficial to you at this given point in your life. It may be worthwhile to note that the passage chosen for one's meditation ought not to be too long, for the point of using Scripture for prayer is not the same as Bible reading. Bible reading is certainly a laudable exercise in its own right but it is not meditation. Ideally one needs only two or three verses of Scripture on which to meditate. The purpose of the Scripture is to act as a trigger for the quiet listening to the God-within who is the point of it all. Allow the words to sink in and touch the core of your being, and out of that core will emerge the voice that will once again speak personally to your heart. And this voice is always one of love, for it is the voice of the God-within. Love does not mean an absence of conflict or negative feelings; it means that you can experience them in the context of a relationship that accepts you for who you are and does not condemn or judge.

Once I knew a retreatant who had a profound experience of God. She ended up spending seven to eight hours a day for eight days on just one passage of Scripture. It alone was enough, for it transported her into places where words ceased to have meaning, the experience of love was so great. She had started her retreat by meditating on the words of the prophet Isaiah:

Do not be afraid for I am with you.
I have called you by name. You are mine (Is 43:2).

These words were enough. She got caught up in them, and in the powerful week of prayer that followed God filled her with numerous blessings and consolations, accompanied by bounteous tears of love so that she had no need to go on to any other Scripture passage. A short phrase or sentence, therefore, is the ideal way to meditate on Scripture. Perseverance with that passage, even though initially one may find it unresponsive, can bring great rewards. But again, a caution. If, after giving yourself to the particular passage, persevering with it, and genuinely being open to the working of God in it, you find no movement—either negative or positive—taking place, move on to another passage the next time you pray. There is no substitute for common sense in prayer, or in our daily lives!

What then, in summary, is the procedure to engage in for meditating on Sacred Scripture? Let me outline it as follows. (1) Begin by going to your place of solitude and becoming still inside and out. Closing your eyes helps as does getting into a comfortable posture. (2) When you feel recollected, pick up your Bible and go to the pre-chosen Scripture passage and read it through slowly. I say pre-chosen, because if you were to try to find a particular passage at this time your recollection could be interrupted. Find the passage for your prayer then before you settle down to pray. (3) As you read through the passage, listen to what you are feeling. Is there a phrase or a word that touches a responsive chord within you? Do you feel a particular, previously unfelt emotion aroused by the word or phrase? If so, take note of it. (4) Return to that particular word or phrase and listen to the feeling it aroused, resting in the feeling for as long as the feeling is present. It is good to avoid analysis here; merely attend to the feeling, relish it, savor it, let it stand by itself without bringing the intellect to bear on it. (5) Then, when you sense that the feeling is abating, you may wish to simply rest further in its recollection or go on to the next word or passage that attracted you.

It is perhaps worth repeating that negative feelings toward certain words or passages are not good nor bad; they are just feelings. By staying with the feeling you could well discover a truth or a lesson, or an insight that words alone, or intellectual reasoning alone, may not have revealed to you. Positive feelings are likewise to be attended to, but need little comment, for the joys they bring speak for themselves, and one experiencing such joy needs little encouragement to persevere. Of course, the dry times previously mentioned also come. Persevere, wait patiently, and in the waiting can come a gift that will in itself bring its own reward. It can be in itself an affirmation of one's belief that the God-within is certainly present but is allowing the pray-er to be on his or her own for a while. This could be either to test one's commitment, or to show the pray-er who gives the gifts of peace and joy, or perhaps because the pray-er was lazy and slothful and did not fully enter into the prayer, hence defaulting the experience of love through his or her own fault. *The Spiritual Exercises of St. Ignatius* can be very helpful here for discerning these various movements. See especially annotations #313-336 on the "Rules for the Discernment of Spirits." It would be better not to read them but rather have a person versed in them apply the rules to you in your own particular situation and explain them to you in that context. But if there is no such person around, reflect on them yourself, with the caution that the sixteenth century language and culture in which it was written should not be allowed to obviate the insightful truths that these "Rules" provide. It is best to get a modern translation of the book for this purpose, therefore. I highly recommend David Fleming's translation that can be readily obtained by writing to the Institute for Jesuit Sources, Fusz Memorial, 3700 West Pine Blvd., St. Louis, Mo. 63108. Another book I would recommend is one that deals very well with negative feelings toward God. It is *May I Hate God?* by Pierre Wolf (Paulist Press, 1979). It has the additional advantage of having lists of Scripture texts for prayer in time of suffering in its appendix.

In conclusion let me share with you a few of my own favorite Scripture passages for your prayer:

Old Testament

Lv 26:11–13	Jb 38:1–11	Lam 3:22–33
Dt 1:29–32	Jb 42:1–6	Ez 36:24–28
Dt 7:7–9	Is 40:1–8	Hos 11:1–4
Dt 32:10–12	Is 41:10–13	Mi 6:8
1 Kgs 19:9–13	Is 43:1–3	Zeph 3:14–20
Jdt 9:11–12	Is 55:1–13	
The Psalms	Jer 29:11–14	

New Testament

Lk 1:46–55	Jn 1:35–39	Lk 18:35–43
Lk 2:1–14	Mk 10:13–16	Lk 24:1–8
Mt 5:1–12	Lk 7:44–50	Rom 8:31–39
Mt 7:7–11	Jn 8:3–11	1 Cor 13:4–13
Mk 1:40–45	Jn 11:24–27	Eph 3:14–21
Mt 11:28–30	Lk 15:20–24	Phil 2:6–11
Mt 14:22–33	Lk 18:9–14	1 Jn 4:7–21

Dream Prayer

All of us dream. It is said that during an average night we have four to five significant dreams. Most of us do not remember these dreams and so we say that we don't dream, or that we dream rarely. But dreams are very much a part of who we are and can become a very significant source of self-understanding. In recent times, beginning with Sigmund Freud, and developed greatly by C. G. Jung, we have been exposed to a new understanding and respect for dreams and their potential to help us. They can help us get in touch with that "collective unconscious" within us that speaks truth in a way our conscious state is rarely permitted to do, and in that encounter meet the God-within in a startling way. In the last few years the value of the dream has been further described by the works of Morton Kelsey, a student of C. G. Jung, who has made an invaluable contribution to the value of dreams as a way to listen to God in his book *God, Dreams and Revelation: A Christian Interpretation of Dreams* (Augsburg Publishing House, Minneapolis, 1974) as well as his popular introductory work, *Dreams: A Way To Listen to God,* (Paulist Press, N.Y., 1978).

It has only been a few years since I have started working with my dreams and even less since I have started praying over them and recommending this form of dream praying to my directees. I have been astonished at the results. For most of my life I treated dreams with the same skepticism that my peers did. They were seen as merely unconscious rehashings of the previous day's events, or entertaining pieces of nocturnal fiction that provided amusement in the retelling, but little else. To this day most scholars I talk to see dreams as little more than this and tend to scoff at any real significance in them.

Yet, even though I initially agreed with them, it was an area that I frequently found fascinating, and occasionally frightening. I then had the good fortune of meeting some Jesuits who were clinical psychologists and spiritual directors as well, who told me that they direct retreats based solely on the dreams of their retreatants with amazing results. This got me even more interested in the potential for dreams being avenues of contact with God, and I started recording my dreams, using them for prayer, and allowing God to touch me through them. The results proved more than worth the effort. I started reading the popularly available material on the subject and then investigated the more extensive and scholarly writings of C. G. Jung on the subject. I became increasingly convinced that I had been missing out on a prayer form that could put me in touch with the God-within much faster and with a greater facility than the traditional prayer forms of the Church. With the help of Morton Kelsey's writings, though, I came to realize that hearing God speak in dreams was nothing innovative and in fact was very much a part of both Old and New Testament writings. Some of the most important communications of God with his people, in fact, were done through dreams. To cite a few examples, we have the dreams of Jacob and Moses' visionary experiences, as well as Nathan the prophet and Solomon, all well encapsulated in the writings of Joel, especially Joel 3:1 where the outpouring of God's spirit is evidenced when "your sons and daughters shall prophesy, your old men shall dream dreams, and your young men shall see visions." Then, in the New Testament writings we have the well-known dreams of Joseph and the wise men, and the dream Pilate's wife had about Jesus. Then there are the events of the first Pentecost and the various actions of the apostles following this outpouring of the Holy Spirit that were often aided by dreams and visions. The accounts of Peter and Paul frequently mention instances of God communicating with them through dreams and visions, words that in the Greek can refer either to a sleeping dream, a waking vision, or a sleeping vision.

Dreams have also played a quite significant role in the early Church, and it was only with the writings of St. Thomas Aquinas and its emphasis on speculative thinking about God and the things of God that dreams and all other non-verifiable realities started to be neglected. With the coming of the Enlightenment and the modern age of scientific investigation the world of dreams became further neglected, and it is only in this century, especially thanks to C.G. Jung, that we have attempts being made to reverse this trend and recognize once again the potential significance of dreams in our lives.

Before one attempts to pray on one's dreams it is necessary to know something about dreams. C. G. Jung in his *Collected Works* notes that

the unconscious is not just a receptacle for all unclean spirits and other odious legacies from the dead past. . . . It is in very truth the eternally living, creative, germinal layer in each of us, and though it may make use of age-old symbolical images it nevertheless intends them to be understood in a new way (Morton Kelsey, *God, Dreams and Revelation,* p. 200, quoting C. G. Jung, *Collected Works,* Vol. 4, p. 330).

Dreams tell stories that can range from brief interludes to lengthy complex dramas filled with many characters and events. It is very important to note that no matter who the characters may be in the dreams they are all facets of my own being. I am not dreaming about other people, but rather I am dreaming about parts of my very own psyche that those people in my dream represent. The first question to pose to oneself then, when attempting to pray on one's dreams is: What facet of me is that person in my dream representing? And what is significant to me about that facet? Now it is at times quite difficult to interpret the significance and the meaning of the people in one's dream, but if one has difficulty, consulting an expert can often help elucidate the meaning inherent in it.

Further, there are dreams that have no real significance personally but nevertheless make an impact. These are dreams that contain what Jung calls archetypal forms, symbols that are present in our unconscious and reveal images that can speak to us of the very core of our being and hence can effectively reveal the God dwelling within in a most eloquent way.

Jung isolated these archetypal images and described them in detail. Of the vast array three stand out as most important. They appear and reappear in one form or another in everyone's dreams. They are: the shadow, the animus, and the anima. The shadow is a dark and threatening figure representing the undeveloped, uncivilized and primitive part of us. The animus and the anima are the male and female aspects to be found in every man and woman. The male aspects in a woman or the female aspects in a man are those aspects of one's personality most different and strange from one's conscious personality. So, a man who deeply appreciates and values the fine arts, natural beauty, his own good looks, and the like is expressing his anima, while an aggressive and dominating woman, or one who deals with abstractions, is revealing her animus. If one chooses to pray on one's dreams, bringing to consciousness these conflicting facets of one's personality, great harmony can be facilitated, for each of these opposing facts contains within itself sources of immense satisfaction and wholeness if it is well integrated into one's conscious personality. It should be repeated that there are numerous archetypes; these are only three of the most common. Investigating them and allowing them to reveal their meaning can put one in touch with the God-within and result in a greater joy and freedom than perhaps one ever thought possible.

What does one do when one decides to pray on one's dreams? First, begin to record the events of your day before going to sleep. Then, start recording the dreams. The commonest complaint here is: How can I do that? I never even remember my dreams! I felt the same way initially. I was told to simply tell myself just before I went to sleep that "tonight I am going to remember my dreams." I did, though admittedly with some skepticism. When I awoke in the morning I had remembered one dream. I wrote it down on a pad I had bought for the purpose. The next day I repeated my command to myself and remembered only one dream again. I recorded it. But as the days went by I soon found that I was remembering three, four and even five dreams a night. It takes perseverance, and the more one does it the easier it becomes.

I think it is very helpful to first talk to someone who knows about dreams and their value or to do some reading for yourself before praying over them. Use either the writings of C.G. Jung, or, in a non-technical and hence more palatable form, the works of Morton Kelsey already mentioned.

The next stage is to pray over them. Do this by going over the recorded events of your day as well as your dreams. When you actually pray over them treat your dreams as a direct revelation by God to you, somewhat like using the Bible for meditation, and see whether you recognize any connection between your day's events and your dreams. Then, become very still, ask the God-within to be present to you, and reveal to you what he wants you to learn from the characters in your dream, and the dream as a whole. Now listen to what you feel about each of the characters, and using your intellect ask yourself what this particular action in the dream means for you. Then have a dialogue with yourself and with the God-within about what you are feeling. Record your conclusions.

Finally, I think it is very important to have someone you can talk to about your dream. It should be someone who knows you well and is aware of your whole life situation. Experts, of course, are hard to come by, but someone you trust, who has common sense, and hopefully some training as a psychologist or a spiritual director, could prove very helpful.

Dreams reveal to us the affairs of our heart with a directness that the language in the head can rarely accomplish. They go beyond words and reveal to us truths about ourselves, our attitudes and feelings, that years of intellectual ruminating cannot accomplish. If we choose to use this prayer form we are choosing to encounter God face to face. While the truths it reveals may be disconcerting, the consequences make it immensely worthwhile. For the more we are in touch with the truth within, the more we can become integrated as human beings, and the peace and harmony that that breeds will give us the confidence to face whatever travails may await us with a courage and a confidence that we would never have had before.

Fantasy Prayer

One of the most delightful ways of entering into the core of one's being and finding there an "eternal Minister" is through using the faculty of one's imagination.

Once again there are obstructions to using this prayer form effectively. If we can let go of them we can find in this prayer a place of genuine enjoyment and true consolation.

The first of the obstructions comes from our social conditioning. We tend to argue against play in our lives, or at any rate against child's play. After all we are not kids anymore, are we? It is not appropriate for us to play cops and robbers as adults, and certainly it doesn't make sense to "reduce" something as sacred as prayer time to adventuring through our imaginations, and so on. It doesn't make rational sense, we argue, and if we want to enter fully into our humanity we certainly ought not to be playing fantasy games. This is the second obstruction—allowing our minds alone to dictate our reasoning over matters that frankly do not belong to the domain of the mind. For the human person is not only intellect, he or she is also many other things, each different, each important in its own way, all combined in a delicately balanced network that is the human person. All of our faculties can be utilized to reach the core of our humanity, and this certainly includes the faculty of one's imagination.

If one chooses to use this method one is immediately opening a veritable pandora's box of delights and adventures. The options are limitless, limited only by one's own imagination. Dare to dream and one may be astonished how quickly one's dream can lead one into the core of one's existence. For the imaginary story one may choose to follow can evoke an array of feelings that in turn can quickly surface truths that intellectual reasoning would arrive at only after a long and tedious process.

How does one fantasize in prayer? Begin by first employing the usual prerequisites for quietening down and becoming still. Then begin to picture a place that you may be especially attracted to, have Jesus enter the scene and let your imagination take over. Let's do one right now as I write.

I am sitting at my desk, trying to share with you what I am feeling in my heart. I am not sure whether I am being clear enough . . . I pause . . . Now I invite Jesus to enter my room and sit by me . . . I sense his presence. I don't try to picture him or see his face. That could become a distraction. I merely sense his presence by my side and listen to what I am feeling . . . I pause for a few moments relishing the feeling. I ask the Lord to join me for a walk outside. We walk into the garden and slowly take a stroll among the bushes and the vines growing on the fence. I am reminded of his words, "I am the vine, you are the branches." I let myself feel the gratitude for being so closely identified with him . . . I tell him so . . . I sense his responsive smile . . . I listen to my feelings. It is a beautiful day, fresh after a summer rain . . . We walk on a little further . . . He points to a beautiful flower, then bends down, breaks it, and gives it to me . . . I thank him, somewhat surprised. Then he touches the stem from which he had broken the flower. Immediately another flower, even more beautiful than the first, blooms on it . . . I listen to my incredulity. He smiles and points to the end of our path which runs at the top of a slight hill overlooking the city. We walk up to its edge and look over the city . . . He invites me to go down to it with him . . . We now take the path that winds down the hillside to the city . . . After some time we get down to the main road . . . It is by a small shopping center. We walk through the shopping center . . . There are some young kids on bicycles riding around the parking lot . . . He hails them. They stop. He tells them to be careful because the cars sometimes drive too fast around that parking lot . . . They laugh at him and one of them tells him that they know quite well how to negotiate the fast cars. He feels hurt. How do you feel? Then suddenly a car comes off the street straight at the kids. They quickly cycle out of the way and shout an obscenity at the driver. The driver, a young high school age adult, slams on the brakes. He quickly revs up his engine and making a sharp circle chases the kids who start bicycling away furiously. He catches up with them and deliberately clips the rear wheel of the last cyclist's bike. The kid goes flying into the air and falls with a thud. Jesus and I run to his side . . . He is unconscious, with a nasty cut on his forehead. It was the kid who had told Jesus he knew well how to negotiate the fast cars. Jesus touches him. He opens his eyes, completely healed . . . Jesus helps him up and tells him to go on home. Shaken, he starts walking away silently, then all of a sudden turns around and says, "Thank you." Then he walks away . . . I tell Jesus that I feel humbled to have been with him this afternoon and to have seen him work miracles. He says he feels humble and grateful to me for wanting to be with him this afternoon. Then he says "Thank you" to me . . . He now says that he has to be going on . . . We say goodbye and he walks away.

Slowly bring yourself back to the present. What are you feeling, what are you thinking? In your present feelings, and in the feelings you had as you accompanied me on my fantasy walk with Jesus, he was speaking to me and to you. Do you feel the effect of his non-verbal communication? Do you feel any different from what you were feeling at the start of the fantasy?

The Lord becomes immediately accessible to us through our fantasy. The more we use it the more we can experience his presence within us, and derive from that the insight and the hope to go on. Two books that have several excellent fantasy prayers that I would recommend are: *Quiet Places with Jesus* by Rev. Isaias Powers, C.P. (Twenty-Third Publications, P.O. Box 180, Mystic, Conn. 06355) and *Sadhana: A Way to God* by Anthony de Mello, S.J. The former contains forty guided imagery meditations that can provide an excellent start for you, and the latter contains eighteen of some of the most profound fantasy prayers I have made. Making use of them can open for you a doorway to your inner self and to God who dwells there that will offer you an entirely new perspective on yourself and God.

The Prayer of Memory

In the fast-paced world we live in our lives can all too often be taken up with the affairs of the present moment. So much "happens" in a given day, so many immediate concerns present themselves to us that we can lose touch with our past. Yet we are a people with a story. Each one of us has a personal history and in that history is an inexhaustible resource for discovering not only our truest selves but also the God who has been a participator in that history from the beginning of our time on this earth, and even before. We are not created in a vacuum. We didn't just happen; we have a distinct origin, and from that distinct origin we have developed through a series of experiences, and continue to do so.

The prayer of memory invites us to remember these experiences. It calls us to go back in time, using the faculty of our memory and deliberately reliving those experiences, hence making them available once again to us, enabling, in the process, a perspective to develop on our present moment in history that can vastly expand and enrich our understanding of ourselves. It was this belief in the significance of memory that gave the Hebrew people access to divine revelation. For them history was so very important because in it was to be found God's will. Listening to the events of their history and "remembering" them is what gave them the profound insights into God's nature and his covenantal love, and consequently directed the actions of their lives in the present and into the future.

But this is not mere recollection. It is prayer. Hence, as in all prayers, it is not an exercise done alone but rather done in companionship with the God within. Further, it is more a reliving than a remembering in the English sense of the word. This means that one recreates, as best one can, the total scenario of the particular memory one may be entertaining. Hence it calls us to picture the details of the place, the clothing and the scents or smells, the colors on the walls, or, if it is an outdoor memory, the trees and plants, the mood of the sky and the like. It calls us to actually remake the event through our memory, and then simply go through the whole scene, getting in touch with our own feelings there and allowing those feelings to become present once again. It is important not to analyze or criticize the event being remembered but rather to let the event speak for itself in the remembering.

There are essentially two types of events that we remember—sad times and happy times. In both memories try to find God's presence in the event. I mean, as you listen to your feelings in the reliving, try to discover what they are telling you. Dialogue with the God-within about them and see whether you can discover the gift that that particular event brought you. In the recognition of the gift is contained the recognition of God's presence.

But this could be difficult to do if one is reliving a painful memory. How can God be present in the reliving of one's divorce, let us say, or the untimely death of a loved one—there is no such thing as a timely death after all!—or the reliving of a horrible accident, and the like? How can one relive such memories and find a God of peace and justice in them, let alone a God of love?

And then there are painful memories that we may have successfully repressed. I remember a friend I was once directing having to come to terms with some very

51

painful childhood memories of rejection and insecurity. She was not initially aware of how much her present insecurity was being influenced by her past. I asked her to try the prayer of memory. She agreed. I suggested that she return to specific childhood memories, and relive them, but with a difference. "Invite Jesus into the painful experience," I said, "and as you relive it dialogue with him about your feelings, and see him with you, holding you by the hand throughout the experience, whispering words of encouragement and support as you endured the pain. Don't go on to the next painful memory till you feel his consoling embrace and caring love, and till you are at peace over it, having forgiven all who harmed you in it." After a few weeks I talked with her again. She described her experience as follows: "Initially I was terrified of going back into a territory of myself that I did not want to go back to at all. Once I let Jesus go with me into it, though, I felt a little safer. I let him lead me there, going back and experiencing the suffering that I had denied and repressed. With Jesus present I gradually sensed that a significant part of myself that I had sealed up in a tomb was set free." That has been some time ago now. Her new freedom developed and has expressed itself through many creative works. She said that being freed of her repressed childhood memories was the reason she feels she can now do art work again—something she had not been able to do for a long time. In that she has discovered the gift in the pain. She has found God in a new way in her life.

I believe that in every painful memory there is a lesson. The "death" that the memory evokes also contains in it a word for "life." If we can go beyond the pain and ask ourselves what that pain has taught us we can quite possibly discover an important lesson about ourselves, about life itself, and about God. I don't believe our God is out to get us. It is hard for me to imagine a God who sent his only Son to free us from the shackles of our sins being vindictive and punitive in his treatment of us. That, unfortunately, is the God many of us grew up with—One sitting in judgment from on high and waiting with raised hand to strike us down with a retributive hand the moment we err. I feel that is an underdeveloped and somewhat uneducated view of God. It gives God a bad name! I also have difficulty with the concept of a God who lets bad things happen to people, and then expects the people to say, in the midst of their anguish and sorrow, that it is God's will. In an insightful and humorous book, *The Un-original Sinner and the Ice-Cream God* by John Powers there is correspondence between a young boy and a gas station owner who doubles as God. In one of those letters, the young boy, Conroy, asks God, "What do people mean when they say it is God's will?" The answer God gives is: "I don't know. I never felt the need to write one."

Many painful events are described by many good people as being God's will. And the unspoken inference from this is, "Accept it, for there is nothing you can do about it anyway." Holy resignation is the hoped-for consequence. But resignation, for it to be holy, has to contain an awareness of uniqueness, one's set-apartness in God's eyes. It is hard to believe that God has set us apart to suffer needlessly. Suffering is a very valuable part of human growth provided the sufferer can learn what the gift is in the suffering. Once we can get in touch with the gift and the hope that the suffering brought us we can truly begin to allow our resignation to become holy. If we do not reflect on the pain, however, and superficially write it off as God's will we could very easily become angry, and then bitter, and quite apart from discovering God's will in it we could close ourselves off from God himself. And that would be a tragedy, for we would be effectively cutting ourselves off from life itself. What does God ask of us? Certainly not a wallowing in suffering, an attempt to "offer up" our wounds to a vengeful God in the hope his anger against us will be appeased. No!

What God asks of us is the sacrifice of a contrite spirit, a humble heart that acknowledges our sinfulness and looks toward him with hope for salvation. In the words of the prophet Micah we are reminded of what God wants of us:

> What is good has been explained to you. This is what Yahweh asks of you: only this, to act justly, to love tenderly and to walk humbly with your God (Mi 6:8).

The Prayer of Memory can enable this to happen and prevent a selfish wallowing in suffering from occurring. It can open up vast stores of insight and understanding within ourselves and it can help us see, with that inner eye, the gift in the pain, Jesus himself in the storm. And in that "sight" we can once again appreciate that we are not alone, that we are not unloved but rather dearly loved and cherished by a God who may challenge his daughters and sons at times but never destroy them. As the author of Hebrews says:

> Suffering is part of your training; God is treating you as his children. Has there ever been any child whose father did not train him? If you were not getting this training as all of you are, then you would not be children but bastards (Heb 12:7).

So, the Prayer of Memory can become an invaluable tool not just for developing a truer perspective on one's contemporary situation but also for understanding with greater insight who one is and who is the God-within that trains one as his own daughters and sons. The Prayer of Memory can also be an excellent way of enjoying your life more today. Relive a past happy experience, deliberately delight in the joy and the lightheartedness of the memory, see Jesus, the God-within, present in it, and find him having a great time there as well. After taking your time about delighting in it, give thanks for the gifts contained in that happy memory, and return to the present moment. It is quite possible that your perception of the present would have changed, so much so that a problem or difficulty you may have been facing prior to the prayer no longer appears as insurmountable, a previous pain no longer as deadly.

What this prayer can do is give one a truer perspective on oneself. It can reintroduce a balance into one's life where previously one may have felt off-balance, either through a pervasive depression over some situation, or simply just feeling blue over nothing in particular. It can, through this "live" rerun of a past happy event, inform one of the truth, that one is loved and cared for, and is never alone.

The steps to it in summary then are as follows: (1) Using the usual techniques, still oneself and enter into your private "cell." (2) Return to a time of either joy or sorrow and relive the experience, allowing the feelings you had at that time to once again surface. (3) Invite Jesus to share the experience with you, dialoguing with him along the way. (4) Thank God for them, no matter what they are, and ask humbly what God wants you to learn out of them. (5) Rest for a while in the lesson, continuing to listen to yourself as you do so. (6) Relish the feelings evoked.

Contemplation

Have you ever been in love? I don't mean the adolescent sort that is so popular in mass media presentations, the kind that equates love with selfish good feelings and sexual gratification. By being in love I mean the genuine care and patience, the tenderness and perseverance, the caress of selfless caring that love in its more mature expression offers. Love—the word itself stirs so many emotions, each emerging out of a personal history that is as private as the intimate memories have been. Love, with all the hopes and dreams for happiness that it promises and the lived reality of it frequently contradicting the ideal, can remind us of our failures and deceits, and also of our own most profound joys and fulfillments. Love—does it not spark an eternal desire within us for its completion? Is there not a longing for a true union, an intertwining of minds, hearts, bodies, dreams that will result in a complete freeing that is at once self-affirming and self-effacing? I think, if anything, that the current breakup of relationships answers a resounding "yes" to the question. Yes, people in a society dehumanized at times to an extreme are yearning for an honest, open human encounter of genuine love. The breakup of relationship after love relationship reflects the yearning for a love true and steadfast, one that lasts through adversity as well as triumph. Yet are we not a hope-filled society? For in each breakup, in each anguish-steeped shattered dream, does not a hope emerge for yet another "love" that all too often proves as plastic as the one just dispensed with? We may pause and ask: Why? How could he have done it to me, how could she have walked away? And the wail, the far-too-common wail, once again arises "Oh . . . oh where is love?" echoing the words of the little waif, Oliver. In fact, in our wait we can find a solace—a heartfelt experience of identification not only with the immediate experience of failure but with the popularized Dickensian character that somehow puts us in a position of self-righteous anguish. Yet it does not last. We return to the grim reality of the present moment, and here in this present time we look at ourselves in a mirror and perhaps say with a resoluteness, imagined or genuine, that we will live to love again.

But is this the process of love? Despite Shakespeare's insightful and accurate observation that "The course of true love ne'er did run smooth," is this the course of love? Is this love? The question has been posed in so many ways over the centuries that one weakens at the thought of posing it again, unless one has an answer that has been offered in as many ways, and in as many centuries.

Love is a very dark stream flowing in the inmost recesses of one's being as Teilhard de Chardin says, silent yet alive, powerful yet gentle, a source of unexplainable energy leading to ecstatic delight and woeful depression. Love is, as the saying goes "a many-splendored thing," though, of course, it can also be a many-forked thing. Love evokes cries of delight, cries of equal anguish. Love is what makes us most alive, and as the song goes we are "born to be alive." So, to be alive, that is to love. Yet we don't know it! Infuriating as it may be, we cannot encounter it in a fleeting moment, with the flick of a switch. It takes time—and in a time-conscious environment that can be a disqualifier. Nevertheless, that is what it takes—time. And it takes a willingness to descend into the lower depths and there discover not a bright light, but a stream, a dark stream that is incomprehensible, as the anonymous author of long ago so well put it in *The Cloud of Unknowing*. This is the title of the book I recommend for further developing what I say here. It is available in a newly edited version with an introduction by William Johnston (Doubleday, Image Books, 1973).

Love is a yearning on the part of one human being for another. In contemplative prayer one human being yearns for a love relationship, and ultimately a union with the infinite God. It is the quintessential joining of hearts and minds that fulfills the ultimate longings of the human being for infinite love. It begins when one recognizes a deeply-felt longing for God, a longing that stirs out of the darkest recesses of one's being and is expressed at times with a sigh that involves the whole body. It calls for undivided attention to the Beloved so yearned for, to the point of setting aside all thoughts about anything else, even holy and comforting reflections and words. It is the total dedication to the Beloved alone, obviating even thoughts about the Beloved's work. It is like entering a blacked-out room where your beloved awaits you, and without seeing him or her you sense, in the darkness, the presence of your love and in that sensing derive an all-embracing affirmation of all you are.

Let us now turn to a consideration of contemplation that I trust will be helpful for you to enter into this prayer form.

In the words of the unknown author of that spiritual classic, *The Cloud of Unknowing,* this is how you go about contemplation:

> Lift up your heart to the Lord, with a gentle stirring of love desiring him for his own sake and not for his gifts. Center all your attention and desire on him and let this be the sole concern of your mind and heart. Do all in your power to forget everything else, keeping your thoughts and desires free from involvement with any of God's creatures or their affairs whether in general or in particular (*The Cloud of Unknowing,* Ch. 3).

It is important to note that contemplative prayer is not something one can just decide to do one day. It has to be a response to an invitation made by the God-within to become involved with him intimately. It has been said that contemplative prayer is a higher form of prayer than meditation, but I think it is "higher" only because the invitation of God to this very personal and intimate love relationship with him alone is heard only by a few. And even fewer succeed in responding to it because of the struggles inherent in stilling oneself to such an extent that all distractions cease. Also, it requires little effort or planning on the part of the pray-er other than the effort needed to concentrate on the Beloved alone. It is difficult to an extreme to seek God alone, to "Think of God as he is in himself," and even if the desire is there the method is hidden, even as the method of two human beings becoming united in love is hidden. For how can love expressed in profound union ever be adequately outlined in a methodology, as the author of *The Cloud of Unknowing* so succinctly states in response to his rhetorical question "How shall I proceed to think of God as he is in himself?" He replies, "I do not know."

What does one do then, presuming the desire for God is present? "Abandon all thoughts and cover them with a cloud of forgetting. Then let your loving desire step bravely and joyfully beyond them and reach out to pierce the darkness above," that is, the cloud of unknowing.

This abandoning of all thoughts is where the effort comes in, for many are the distractions that try to get us to look elsewhere than at the Beloved. The ensuing conflict, between surrendering to the yearning and giving in to the distractions, is where the work comes in. The temptation can become great to just give up, and even though a glimpse of the profound joy that is available to us is seen in the longing itself, the path to it appears almost too difficult to tread. Perseverance is essential, coupled with a strong faith that assures the pray-er that since God has invited, he will help the pray-er savor the fruits of his love.

One may argue, however, that if God is so keen on union with me, why does he not make it easy for me. He wants to, but he needs our help. And he will help if we choose to engage in the struggle to get rid of the many distractions our thoughts provoke. God awakens the love in the yearning we have for him alone; then we respond by doing our best to still our thoughts, confident that he is helping us the while.

It is important to persevere, and gradually one will find that it is getting easier in that you will begin to enjoy more the inner joy it produces. As is written in *The Cloud of Unknowing:* "As time goes by, however, you will feel a joyful enthusiasm for it and then it will seem light and easy indeed" (Ch. 26).

But how does one still one's thoughts? Let me suggest a way that works for me. It is important, first of all, not to battle the thoughts. Struggling to get rid of them begins, paradoxically enough, by acknowledging their presence. Then, without becoming alarmed or anxious, set them aside by simply saying a word, such as "Jesus" or "God" or, as is advised in *The Cloud of Unknowing,* say "love" or a similar word that works for you. This brings you back to the yearning and the prayer continues. In a single prayer time one may have to do this several times over, but what happens is that the more one does it, the easier it becomes till eventually the distractions become few and far between, and you will be more and more taken up with the delight of being loved by God himself. It is important to "learn to be at home" in the darkness of the wait and in the gentle handling of the distractions and soon you will begin to experience deeply God's intimate and very personal love for you.

What do I get out of all this effort? An experience of love that can be so affirming and so enjoyable that all else—the struggles and problems, the prejudices and insults we all endure—become quite insignificant. Our perspective on the world around us changes, and we can begin to look upon even our enemies with an understanding and a benevolence that wouldn't have seemed possible before. It brings you alive to the needs of others, and compassion flows from that awareness, making it easily possible to reach out to the sister or brother in your midst who is in want. Then the one wounded, you can heal, for your presence itself will become a healing presence, and your generosity will overflow, until you can indeed be accused of being a fool for Christ by the world you live in. And that will make it all worthwhile!

Centering Prayer

This is a contemporary wording for the prayer described in *The Cloud of Unknowing.* Yet it isn't quite the same as contemplation, as you will see. It was initially used by Thomas Merton, that great contemporary master of prayer and spirituality, and it has recently been developed and clearly articulated by M. Basil Pennington, O.C.S.O. in his fine book, *Centering Prayer: Renewing an Ancient Christian Prayer Form* (Doubleday & Co., Inc., 1980).

In this work Father Basil offers us a three-rule formulation of the method of centering prayer. Its new name, incidentally, derives from Thomas Merton's observation that "monastic prayer begins not so much with 'considerations' as with a 'return to the heart,' finding one's deepest center . . ." (*Centering Prayer,* p. 42). It is a name that quite effectively describes both the direction of the prayer—moving toward one's center—as well as the point of the prayer—encountering one's center where the God-within dwells.

It is perhaps necessary to note that when I speak of God dwelling in a particular place, it is not a physical location to which I am referring. It is an attempt to articulate an inner Presence that can be experienced and attended to through the faculty of our hearts. Again, the word heart here does not, of course, mean the physical muscle that keeps us alive; rather the word seeks to describe, using this physical reality, that "place" where the non-corporeal dimension of ourselves—the feelings, the moods, the affections, and the like—exist. Invisible, yet very real.

Now to the three rules of Father Basil.

Rule One consists of becoming still and quietening down, then gently becoming aware, through one's faith, of God dwelling within. It is a sensing of the presence of Love that can be facilitated by articulating your faith in his presence to you. You could say something like: "Father, I thank you for being so near to me. Please let me become aware of your closeness, and give me what I need to attend to you for these next few minutes." Keep the prayer simple, and let it come from within yourself. Make up your own prayer, and feel free to create new words. The point is to become aware of God already present to you and ask him to give you the gift you need to become present to him. I think if we can first acknowledge that he is already present and yearning for us, it is easier to become present to him. He is the initiator; we respond to his loving invitation. Now we enter into a state of quiet and gentle awareness of God's presence, dwelling as it were in the center of our being. But we will have difficulty remaining there, for many are the distracting thoughts that will come to tempt us away from this quiet and loving attending to God.

Hence, there is the Second Rule, which is the prayer word. It doesn't much matter what the word is. Sometimes I find myself saying "Jesus," the Jesus Prayer that is historically so much an intrinsic part of centering prayer, or "Father" or "God" or "love." It does not even have to be a word; it can be an unintelligible sound, or a sigh. The point of it is to enable you to remain present to your Center. If it accomplishes that, the word or sound you use does not much matter. Further, one word could work one day, another on some other day. Allow yourself the freedom to use the word or sound that best suits you at that particular time.

It is important to use the prayer word gently, and only when needed, that is, when you begin to feel you are drifting away from your Center, and this is the Third Rule. Sometimes several moments may go by before you need it; at other times it could be more frequent. The important thing is not the frequency but the slow, quiet, peaceful, gentle tone with which you say it. That is what returns the pray-er back to the center and away from whatever else one may have become distracted by.

Centering prayer is really quite simple. It consists of being with the Beloved, enjoying, as it were, his company, relishing his presence and delighting in being present to him. I think the prayer allows an attitude to emerge that can transform one's outlook on life. Experiencing the joy of being in the presence of true love has to transform one's outlook, and the more one is present to this God-within the more one will find inner resources and strengths lying hidden, awaiting the presence of an astoundingly intimate love to bring them into the light.

Vocal Prayer

Verbalizing our prayers is the most evident and hence well-known prayer form there is. Until recently most people visualized praying as praying with words. "Saying one's prayers" is a well known phrase and usually meant using words to express one's own or another's thoughts to God. These thoughts encompassed many emotions, such as expressing praise and thanksgiving, petitions, offerings, dedications to God and the like. For example, one of the most popular forms of vocal prayer is the rosary, in which the pray-er is asked to meditate on certain fixed "mysteries" of the life of Christ and his mother Mary, and do so while saying a series of repetitive prayers taken mostly from Scripture. All too often, however, vocal prayers became reduced to an activity that one "had to get in" every day, and prayer, as a consequence, became reduced to a duty that had to be done daily, a task that the sooner accomplished the better so that other more important matters could be attended to. Stories are facetiously told of secret competitions being run in seminaries and convents to see who could get through all fifteen decades of the rosary the fastest! And it was often unclear how one was supposed to pay attention to the words while meditating on a "mystery" that seemed to have little to do with the words themselves. It seemed that if you did one well the other would suffer, and the frequent result would be that neither was done well. The external consequences of this, to an outsider at any rate, would be a group of people going through repetitive prayer exercises as rapidly and as incoherently as possible, paying attention the while to the latest fashions in church or the people coming in late, or apparently just about anything other than what they were purportedly doing, namely praying to God.

Perhaps because vocal prayer of this sort failed to satisfy, perhaps because the changes of Vatican II opened up other avenues of prayer, perhaps because people just reacted against their childhood religious training, or perhaps because prayer just ceased to matter to some, the praying of the rosary, and with it other vocal prayers, fell into disuse. Whatever the reasons many people ceased taking vocal prayer seriously. I think this is most regrettable.

Vocal prayer can be one of the easiest and quickest methods of stilling oneself and entering into a union with God that can truly be affirming. If prayed with devotion vocal prayers can bring one very close to one's center, and facilitate an encounter with the God-within with ease. What is vocal prayer? It is putting into words one's fondest hopes and dreams, using either formulaic and hence familiar sentences, or using words that come to the prayer from within in order to give thanks and praise to God. But it is more than this. It can be a way of stilling one's heart so that the repetitive sentences of the prayer can produce a state of receptive tranquility that in turn can allow distractions to be reduced to a minimum consequenting our alertness to the voice of the God-within that would otherwise be difficult to accomplish. A popular Hinduism of the day is the word mantra, meaning a word or formula recited or chanted designed to induce a state of inner peace and tranquility. The mantra can be an end in itself but it is also used as a means of creating a silent heart. When one can go beyond the words one enters the abode of the God dwelling within; one has entered the core of one's life.

Vocal prayer is also a devout concentration on the words themselves. St. Ignatius of Loyola in his *Spiritual Exercises* describes this method of vocal prayer:

> One may kneel or sit, as may be better suited to his disposition and more conducive to devotion. He should keep his eyes closed, or fixed in one position, without permitting them to roam. Then let him say, "Father" and continue meditating upon this word as long as he finds various meanings, comparisons, relish, and consolation in the consideration of it. The same method should be followed with each word of the "Our Father," or of any other prayer which he wishes to use for this method (Spiritual Exercises, #252).

St. Ignatius then goes on to describe another method of vocal prayer, this involving a measured rhythmical recitation. In this method he says:

> With each breath or respiration one should pray mentally while saying a single word of the "Our Father," or other prayer that is being recited, in such a way that from one breath to another a single word is said. For this same space of time, the attention is chiefly directed to the meaning of the word, to the person who is addressed, to our own lowliness, or the difference

between the greatness of the person and our own lit-
tleness. In this way observing the same measure of
time he should go through the other words of the "Our
Father" (Spiritual Exercises, #258).

Vocal prayer, prayed in these ways, can become a
most rewarding and consoling exercise. It is a method of
prayer that can enable the heart to sing, for it puts one in
a very close union with the God-within. In experiencing
that union one derives a strength and a power to face the
various forces around us that may appear incomprehensible and unfeeling, those forces of this institutionalized
world we live in that so frequently use us as cogs in its
wheels of self-perpetuation.

For an excellent contemporary book of prayers I recommend *A Cry for Mercy* by Henri J. M. Nouwen (Doubleday & Co., Inc., Garden City, New York, 1981). I also recommend the *Scriptural Rosary* published by the Christianica Center, 6 N. Michigan Avenue, Chicago, Illinois
60602. It is an excellent book that is a contemporary ren-
dition of the way the rosary used to be prayed in the Middle Ages. It can be a fine way of returning to praying the
rosary in its more authentic form.

Intercessory Prayer

We are social beings who need one another for our
own sanity. If left alone and in isolation for too long we
can become mentally crippled. Hence one of the worst
forms of torture is not the electric prod or the severe beat-
ings that recalcitrant prisoners are forced to endure; rather
it is putting a prisoner in solitary confinement. Isolation
can tame the human spirit faster than any physical abuse.
It points up in a startling way how much we are depen-
dent on one another for survival.

This holds true in our inner, spiritual lives as well. If all our prayers are self-centered and inward-looking alone it would be better not to pray. If getting in touch with our inmost core does not put us in corresponding touch with the needs and concerns of the sister or brother in our midst we are not yet in touch with our inmost center even though we may believe we are.

One of the easiest ways of determining how you are doing in prayer is to ask yourself how you are doing in loving your neighbor. If one is not becoming more caring and compassionate with one's neighbor, if one continues ignorant and oblivious of the social injustices in one's own community and indeed the world, then one is not truly praying. And there are many who unfortunately claim to be truly praying but who continue as insensitive as they always were to very real injustices around them. These are not bad people—by and large they are very good people—but they have allowed their prayer to be reduced to fulfilling external requirements which, when complete, frees them from feeling any further need to reach out to others with compassion and love. For them prayer has become a duty that once fulfilled asks little else from them.

But if one allows the voice of the God-within to be truly heard one cannot help but go out to others in love, one cannot but reach out to the poor, to the helpless and needy and bring them a healing touch, a firm support. For prayer transforms the pray-er, enabling the pray-er to become so fully human that he or she becomes "a living flame of love" as John of the Cross says so well.

Out of such a transformation there develops a yearning to intercede for others, to ask the God-within to bring healing and hope to a brother or sister in need. Anyone who chooses to embark on a life of prayer is choosing to embark on a process of conversion that has as its end not self-fulfillment but selfless sharing and giving of all one has and is. The yearning to share, to feel with others, begins when one begins to experience the love that the God-within has for you. The more we experience his love for us the more we want to reach out in love to others.

But often we may feel helpless as to how to go about it. It is easy enough to feed the hungry and clothe the naked. That is tangible and can be done either through volunteering one's services at an agency that does that, or contributing financially to it, or even donating our own clothes to it, and the like. But how does one heal a broken heart, or try to offer comfort to one dying in torment, or reach out to an alcoholic who refuses to acknowledge that he or she is indeed one? These are not as easily dealt with as feeding the hungry and clothing the naked.

This is where intercessory prayer comes in. We have experienced how much the God-within loves us, and how much he has supported us when we were depressed and in need. Now it is our turn to ask him to heal another. As is usual the prayer itself is quite simple. One does not need solitude or even much recollection for this prayer. It can be done as effectively in an airplane as in one's room. There is also no need for a set time for it. It can be prayed at any time.

We remember someone, let us say, who is in emotional turmoil or filled with grief. We try to allow our helplessness to aid that person become present to us, and then instead of concentrating on ourselves try to experience the anguish of the other person. Then we simply present the other person to the God-within to be healed. We do this confident that our prayer is being heard and that God in his infinite compassion yearns to heal that person. "Why doesn't he do it then?" one might rightly ask. Because all too often people in anguish have allowed their pain to close themselves off from the possibility of God healing them, and God, not ever interfering with our freedom, respects that. But if we intercede for the person, and take on the pain of the other, we become a conduit as it were that opens up the other to the possibility of healing. And the healing begins not dramatically but simply by being present to the other. The concern on our part can frequently trigger in the wounded person the openness needed for God to heal.

But what if the other is not even aware of our intercessory prayers for him or her? And what if even if the person is aware, nothing happens? Matt and Dennis Linn, in their book *Prayer Course for Healing Life's Hurts* (Paulist Press, N.Y., 1983), note that "we are not promised that everyone we pray for will be changed; what we are promised is that as we reach out to people *we* will be changed and become more whole" (p. 81).

Intercessory prayer is for us as well as for the other. And while we may not find tangible evidence of any change occurring in the other, we may find that changes are occurring in us as we experience a new hope and joy in the God-within who does truly long to save. But this is skirting the issue. What if I don't see any healing taking place in the wounded sister or brother I am praying for?

My own experience in intercessory prayer has been that there *is* a change that takes place in the other. The change, however, is not the one I was wanting or expecting. I remember once praying for a close friend of mine who was struggling intolerably as he watched his own very close friend drift away from him and become increasingly more involved with another. They had been very much in love and he still was, but she had begun to lose interest some months before, and was now having very little to do with him. In fact she wished he would go away and not return. He recounted her words to me in great anguish. I promised I would pray for him and I did. Some months went by, and every time I saw him I asked him how things were between the two of them. "Worse," he replied. "She doesn't want to see me at all anymore."

"Let's keep praying," I said, somewhat uncertain as to what to keep praying for. I prayed for his peace of mind eventually, though also I asked God to bring them back together again if that was for the best. Apparently it wasn't. They didn't get back together. But he started changing. Over a few weeks he started seeing how destructive their earlier relationship had been for both of them. And gradually he began to appreciate himself more, and started sensing a new freedom developing within him. I still see him and when I do I give thanks to God for hearing our prayer, even though our initial petition was not answered; the change for the better in my friend indicated that God's wisdom was clearly greater than ours in the long run. The change we prayed for—the two of them reuniting—did not happen, but what did happen was a new freedom and joy in my friend that emerged out of our intercessory prayer. God does hear our prayers. And even if the change we pray for does not always happen the way we want it to, I am convinced that change does happen, not only in the person we are praying for but in ourselves as well. And the change is for life, for joy and peace, both in ourselves as we intercede for the other, and in the other as he or she allows God to bring healing to the wounded heart, the broken spirit.

Deliverance Prayer

All of us have aspects of our lives in which we are unfree. We may frequently express the wish to ourselves, or even to others, that it would be so good if we could be free of this fear or that habit that controls and binds us. But, just as frequently, we allow the wish to remain just that and continue carrying our burdens for the rest of our days. This could be because we honestly don't know what to do about it, or because we have tried several times to eradicate it from our lives but to no avail, and so just give up trying.

But the one who believes in the power of God working in and amongst his people does have a way of dealing with these un-freedoms and compulsions that a non-believer does not. It is called deliverance prayer. In order to pray it well one first needs to recognize that there truly are forces of evil at work in ourselves as well as in the world around us. Traditionally these forces have been described as evil spirits and, more specifically, as demons.

In a sophisticated, essentially non-spiritual world, in a world that holds verifiable truths as the only yardstick for measuring reality, there is an immediate mental block that can be activated when one hears the words "demons" or "evil spirits." Yet I firmly believe that those who negate this reality in their lives, and reduce it only to psychological problems such as neuroses or psychoses, could very well be avoiding this reality out of a very legitimate fear or anxiety. There is ample evidence available that supports the claim that there are evil forces in and around us that go beyond psychological explanation and diagnosis. Of course, this is not to say that psychology cannot help heal a person of these bonds, but that spiritual deliverance and psychology can be allies here in reducing a person's bonds. If one reduces a person's mental anguish to a psychological problem alone, or, equally, reduces it to the realm of spirituality alone, one could be revealing a quite short-sighted understanding of the human person.

What are some of the bonds from which we would like to be freed? To give you an idea of what I am talking about, simply examine yourself, and honestly try to find those things in you that keep you from being truly free and happy—things such as bad habits, or resentments either toward others or toward an institution, or fears, such as the fear of being oppressed by others or by an unjust social structure, or the fear of never overcoming a sexual problem, and the like, or feelings of anger that can become irrational toward a person or an institution, leading to a real lack of freedom within oneself. Then there is the whole range of evil inclinations produced by feelings of guilt and anxiety that can often compel one to endure intolerable oppression. Most of us, at some time or other in our lives, can identify places of un-freedom within us, and as our lives progress, we may discover that one bondage replaces another, preventing true freedom from ever occurring. It does not take too careful an analysis to determine what in us we would like to be free of.

This is where deliverance prayer can be most helpful. It is grounded scripturally in the Lord's Prayer that Jesus himself prayed, in which the last petition is:

Deliver us from the evil one (Mt 6:13).

It consist of praying to be freed from those forces and powers within us that keep us in chains. Deliverance prayer ideally ought to be done in a community context, and not alone. It should be done by a team of trained professionals that would include a clinical psychologist, a person with the gift of discernment, and people who are effective pray-ers. It is not to be confused with exorcism. I think this is very important to note. It consists of praying for another to be free of those evil spirits within him or her that may be shackling in an oppressive way. It does not deal with demonic possession—that belongs to the full rite of exorcism with all the strict requirements pertaining to that rite, such as receiving the permission of the local ordinary to perform it.

The prayer itself is very simple. The group assembled to pray for the bonded person says,

Spirit of _____,* in the name of Jesus Christ I renounce you, I bind you, and I command you to go peacefully to Jesus Christ now.

This is repeated until the person feels free of his or her particular bonding.

The effects of deliverance prayer, as in all prayer, are not so much to be found in how free the person became during the prayer, but whether the person is more caring and loving of God, of others, and of oneself, after it.

And one must not think that after praying in this way all temptations cease. Far from it. But what happens is that once one experiences God's healing power in one's life, and the important community support that ministers that power, a new confidence and a new freedom develop that enables the person to believe all the more in his or her own worth and importance. It is a prayer that is to be prayed more than once, of course, for all those evil spirits in us have a way of returning time and time again. But with deliverance prayer they can also be driven out time and time again, giving us the chance to choose freedom over bondedness over and over again.

A final point. Can deliverance prayer be done alone? Yes, it can. In fact, although the optimal way is to use this prayer in a community setting, for many the usual way it is done is alone, without any fuss or ceremony. It ought to be prayed in a silent and calm way, in a context of faith, truly believing that the power of the God-within, made so wonderfully visible in the person of Jesus Christ, is stronger than any forces within us for evil and oppression. Further, it can be prayed most effectively if the person praying it genuinely forgives anyone who may have

*Fill in the blank with the name of whatever you are seeking freedom from, such as anger, or depression, a bad habit, and the like.

wronged him or her before entering into the deliverance prayer itself.

In my work as a spiritual director I have often been amazed at the way the Holy Spirit brings freedom and healing to his people. It is evident that being delivered from un-freedom, consequently, is not an uncommon thing, if one truly believes in God's power to free his people. Yet, doubts prevail in all of us. It is necessary to acknowledge them, surrender them to God as a part of us that needs saving, and then proceed with praying for deliverance, confident that God's power is enough to make up for any lack of faith we may have.

An excellent book on deliverance prayer that I recommend for further reading is *Deliverance Prayer* by Matthew and Dennis Linn (Paulist Press, N.Y., 1981). Most of my reflections here I derived from that book, and I urge you to read it through before praying it, for much that is said in it needs to be heard before one attempts this prayer form. But this warning should not dissuade you from praying it, especially for deliverance from minor un-freedoms and burdens. The cautionary note is made only to point out that potential dangers, primarily of self-deception, are present in deliverance prayer, and expert teachers as well as a trained spiritual director are invaluable assets for deriving from this prayer the joys and freedoms it offers. They can also make valuable suggestions to supplement your prayer, and perhaps take away any magical misconceptions about it that some may have. These suggestions could range from proposing that one seek psychological counseling to joining Alcoholics Anonymous to help alleviate the particular bonding one may be experiencing. This would not at all reduce the effect of the prayer itself, but rather augment it through using one's common sense. In an incarnational understanding of God I believe that God is found in many places that we may deem secular and inappropriate for salvation.

Praying for Healing

Central to the ministry of Jesus was healing. Time and time again he would heal the sick, give sight to the blind, make the lame walk again. And he performed the ultimate healing by bringing the dead to life, prefiguring in it his own resurrection from the dead. Central to Christian faith is this mystery of the resurrection, and if we don't believe that we are destined to rise again our faith is a foolish waste of time and energy. But if we do believe it, then we ought to believe in the less ultimate healings that Jesus did, and believe that these healings of the sick, the blind, and the lame take place today as much as they did during the ministry of Jesus.

In a skeptical age this can be difficult to do. Even if example after contemporary example is cited, the skeptic in all of us doubts the authenticity of the healings. "There must be a rational explanation," is our answer, or "I'm sure there is a scientifically verifiable reason for this." But, in fact, the healings that I know of, and have heard about, are quite unexplainable scientifically, and have no rational explanation at all for them.

I think some of our skepticism can perhaps be dealt with by understanding what it means to pray for healing in Jesus' name. First, it means that we believe that God can heal his people, that that is not a fiction. And I mean here not just psychic healing, the easing of a tension or the calming of an anxiety, but actual physical healing of a verifiable ailment. Second, it is very important that we recognize that healing the whole person does not necessarily call for the elimination of a physical ailment, for many great people have become healers themselves precisely because they carried in them a physical ailment but were healed of the inner turmoil connected to it. I am thinking here, for instance, of the great Helen Keller and Dr. Tom Dooley, and some people I know personally who are healers precisely because their physical incapacities give them an inner strength and power that enables them to heal others. Now healing the physical ailment is not always the ultimate cure, and in fact may work against the healing of the whole person. It can be that the ailment suffered could be of significant benefit for that person; it could be that it is the point of conversion for that person, leading to a happier, more meaningful existence. It could be that surrendering to the Lord in the midst of the pain will be a source of new life and freedom for that person, and not only for that person but for many who come in contact with her or him, who witness the power of God's healing love precisely in the way the sufferer accepts with peace and hope the torment he or she may be in. But this is not to contradict or preclude in any way the fact that God can and does heal, in a physical way, those who pray for healing. It is intended to help broaden one's perspective on healing, and challenge the contemporary myth that healing occurs only when a physical ailment no longer is verifiably present. Occasionally the opposite can be true— the physical ailment is healed but the patient remains quite ill in spirit and becomes eventually an unkind, self-centered retributive malcontent, committed to making life as miserable as possible for all who come in contact with him or her. These are not just the hypochondriacs but also those who act as if the whole world is to blame for the physical misfortune that once befell them. So healing, for it to be whole, ought to include both the body and the spirit of our ailing sister or brother.

Third, it is very important to get involved with the other person, the one suffering. Now it could be that one feels safe praying for someone, at a psychic or physical distance, but to become involved, to empathize with the suffering brother or anguished sister is asking too much. I think this is a contemporary malaise that needs to be quickly stamped out. If we truly believe that God loves us as we are, and is for us no matter what, then it is very important that we love our neighbor with that same acceptance as God loves us; and with a suffering neighbor this means getting involved, feeling with the other, entering into his or her skin. In fact, I believe that true healing begins here, and it is from this self-identification with the pain of the other that the other begins to feel the healing take place. No longer does the patient feel abandoned and alone, lost in a mirage of white sheets and antiseptic needles, but rather he or she experiences the healing touch of another empathetic human being. The actual prayer for healing begins here, in fact, when one can feel with the sufferer, and express the empathy through a loving touch. Being with the person with few or no words can often initiate healing that many words or intellectual platitudes can seldom accomplish. The empathy is sensed, not verbalized, and in its silent expression can speak with an eloquence that transcends words. In this we become Jesus for the person, we become his love. Then I pray with him or her for healing.

The next stage in the prayer comes in a sense of contentment and peace on the part of the person suffering, and an acceptance of Jesus' love for him or her. At this point we have to trust that the Lord will proceed with the healing in his own way. My own experiences of healing have been that the healing takes place later, after I have left, but there are others, probably of greater faith and love than I, who have witnessed the physical healing taking place while they were still present. Matt and Dennis Linn, in their book *Prayer Course for Healing Life's Hurts* (Paulist Press, N.Y., 1982, p. 87) go on to describe the next stages. After praying for about fifteen minutes with a man named Joe, who had a back problem—scoliosis of the back—they asked him, "Is anything happening?" He said, "Well, I'm feeling peaceful. And it hasn't gotten any worse." They go on to observe that these are two gifts easily overlooked but to be watched for—feeling peaceful, and not feeling any worse. Then they asked Joe, "Is there anybody you need to forgive?" He initially said "No" but then thought of three people. As he forgave these people the pain in his back abated and he could move his back freely. This, I believe, is a very important step in praying for healing. It links so well our spiritual and physical sides. It also indicates the close interdependence of one to the other. The final step occurs when the physical ailment disappears; in this instance Joe's backbone readjusted itself perfectly.

It is important to note that, as in Joe's case, healing happens through a process of repeated prayers aiding the healing powers in the body, but it can also happen immediately, with no natural explanation. I remember once praying for a lady who was in an advanced stage of cancer. She did not have very long to live. I visited her in the intensive care unit of the hospital she was in. We prayed together that she be healed of her cancer and especially for her three sons and her husband who were understandably struggling greatly to let her go. We prayed for her that, if God in his loving wisdom wanted her to die, she die peacefully and with her eyes on the God who was calling her to himself. I did not know her personally, and was in fact only in that city for a few weeks, but after I visited her I was very moved by her faith and her joy. Through her pain it was evident that she was at peace, her only concern being for her family. So I continued to pray for her and empathized with her after I left, and had several other people pray for her too.

Months went by before I returned to that city again. When I did I asked how her family was, and whether she had died as peacefully as we had hoped. The answer I received really shocked me. "Died?" my friend repeated, and laughed. "She's not dead; she is in fact very well. She has been home for a few months, and all traces of her cancer have disappeared." I looked at him incredulously. "I don't believe it," I said. "You mean our prayers were answered?" "They sure were," he replied. "Everyone involved with her illness, especially her own family, is convinced it was an answer to our prayers." "What do her doctors say?" I asked. "Not much," he chuckled. "They can't explain it medically."

That was over three years ago. She is doing fine. There are no signs of a recurrence of her cancer. Her sons, who were not exactly church-goers before, are firm believers today, and their family has become very much a closely-knit unit of love. But supposing she had died. What then? I think that all too often we pay only lip-service to our belief that death is not ultimate but rather a passage to eternal life. We may mouth the words but our hearts are not in it. Of course, this makes sense, in a human and natural way. Who wants to see our closest relatives and friends die? Yet they do, and we will. That, after all, is the one thing we can be sure of! But, given its universality, why do we allow death to become the grim reaper rather than the passageway to an eternal and joy-filled existence?

The glory of Christianity is that Jesus Christ, the Son of God, has transformed the meaning of death. No longer is it the end of everything, but rather it is the beginning of a new and abundant life with the Author of Life himself. Grieving over a loved one, a necessary, very healthy, and most human emotion to engage in, if done out of this perspective, can become not just a process of unrelieved sorrow or even despair but rather one filled with hope and joy for our brother or sister now experiencing the fullness of life.

Healing prayer involves the whole person, and sometimes healing can occur in a peaceful and indeed joyful death. The best example of this I know is my own grandmother. For years her active life had been curtailed by being confined to a wheelchair—the result of an amputation caused by gangrene. She was a diabetic and the amputation was the only way to save her life. The last few years of her life were filled with prayer, and sending contributions to various charitable organizations. She was always the model of graciousness and true, caring love. Toward the end of her life she was occasionally ill, though not cripplingly so. Some weeks before she died, I had celebrated the sacrament of the sick with her for, I think, the seventh time, when she asked me, "What am I still doing here? Why doesn't God take me? I'm ready to go." I replied, somewhat uncertainly, "Probably because he needs you to pray for people, maybe to pray for me and my work." She looked at me with a puzzled frown but didn't say anything. She had been healed so many times before through the sacrament of the sick that I figured there was no need to be concerned over her question. I was wrong. I think, in her voicing of the question, she was expressing, for the first time in my hearing, her readiness to go home. The healing of this last anointing was expressed in this readiness.

A few weeks later she grew ill again, for the last time. I was not there but my parents were, together with my aunt, and they started praying with her. The decision had been made by her and my parents that they were not going to return to the hospital and make use of artificial means to keep her alive. She didn't want it, and the indignity it would subject her to was unnecessary. So she was at home, peaceful and content as she allowed the pray-ers around her to soothe her into the waiting arms of her loving God. And just before she slid into unconsciousness for the last time she whispered, "Father, into your hands I commit my spirit." Her healing was complete.

Several other examples can be cited where healing prayer brought genuine physical as well as psychic healing to the sufferer. The God who dwells within longs to heal us of all our infirmities, and if we let him the consequences can so easily be a world not wounded but whole, a world where God will truly be recognized as being with his people, for if we let him,

> He will wipe away all tears from their eyes; there will be no more death, and no more mourning or sadness (Rev 21:4).

Then we will be able to see that the God who dwells so intimately within is truly a God who frees his people for life, and see a courageous triumphing over all inimical forces that in this world try to lead us to death.

Family Prayer

The nuclear community of love is the family. The father, the mother, and the children represent the Kingdom of God on this earth in a way that calls out to the world to stop and listen, to see that mutual love is a possibility in spite of all the evidence to the contrary.

Yet the evidence is there. It cannot be denied. We all know of the rapid changes occurring in the family unit. Many of us have probably been affected by these changes and are struggling to cope with them. The world of the past, where a stable family background was the norm, is no longer the case. Wishing for a return to simpler times, for the harmony and peace of a less complex age, while acting as a temporary though doubtful palliative, does not deal with the issue.

The issue is this: the nuclear family unit, that is, the father, the mother, and the children as a unit, is fast disappearing. Many sociologists are of the opinion that it is disappearing for good. This may very well be the case, but meanwhile do we just stand by and allow the fracture to become worse? I hope not.

What do we do? There are many practical things that we can do, such as being a true friend to those experiencing the anguish of separation or the disintegration of a relationship. This must involve a non-judgmental attitude and a recognition that today's dilemmas cannot be solved by yesterday's answers. This could mean suggesting professional counseling to the couple, or, if that would sound too threatening, suggesting a visit to their pastor or some other religious leader they may know. We could also suggest prayer.

It is very hard to pray when the conflict is in progress. Yet, if prayer is given a chance to work, it can at least change the hostile mood to one of acceptance and tolerance.

There are still many families, however, that are happy and loving, true signs of God's love on this earth. What of them? I believe that their happiness and joy is centered in a love that goes beyond the understanding of love that this world has. I believe it is a love grounded in a recognition of the deep-down spiritual meaning of love that reaches into the heart of our humanity, and, most importantly, a willingness to work on making that love a lived reality in their lives. How does one do this? Prayer is one way that has worked for centuries. I believe it has a power that can cement a family together in a love that can really last for all time.

This prayer does not have to be complex or burdensome. It begins with simple formulas prayed at key moments in the family's day. These are usually times when the family is together, such as upon rising in the morning, around the table at the evening meal, and before retiring at night.

In the morning a brief prayer beginning with the Sign of the Cross, a short Morning Offering, the Lord's Prayer, the Hail Mary, and ending with another Sign of the Cross can be a good beginning. Here are those prayers:

The Sign of the Cross

In the name of the Father and of the Son and of the Holy Spirit. Amen.

The Morning Offering

O Jesus, through the Immaculate Heart of Mary, I offer you my prayers, works, joys, and sufferings of this day in union with the Holy Sacrifice of the Mass throughout the world. Amen.

The Lord's Prayer

Our Father, who art in heaven,
hallowed be thy name,
thy kingdom come;
thy will be done
on earth as it is in heaven.
Give us this day our daily bread;
and forgive us our trespasses
as we forgive those who trespass against us;
and lead us not into temptation,
but deliver us from evil.
For thine is the kingdom
and the power
and the glory
forever and ever. Amen.

The Hail Mary

Hail Mary, full of grace,
the Lord is with thee.
Blessed art thou amongst women
and blessed is the fruit of thy womb, Jesus.
Holy Mary, mother of God,
pray for us sinners,
now and at the hour of our death. Amen.

Then conclude with another Sign of the Cross.

The prayer around the table at the evening meal can again be a short prayer asking God to bless the food and one another. Here is the short prayer for this:

> Bless us, O Lord, and these your gifts which we are about to receive through Christ our Lord. Amen.

After the meal a short prayer of thanks can again bond the family by reminding them of God's generosity and goodness. Here is the concluding prayer:

> We give you thanks, Almighty God, for these and all your gifts through Christ our Lord. Amen.

The next time for family prayer is before retiring at night. This could be a little longer in duration and in addition to beginning with the Sign of the Cross, the Lord's Prayer and the Hail Mary, include the following prayers:

The Apostles' Creed

> I believe in God, the Father Almighty,
> Creator of heaven and earth,
> and in Jesus Christ, his only Son, our Lord,
> who was conceived by the Holy Spirit,
> born of the Virgin Mary
> suffered under Pontius Pilate,
> was crucified, died and was buried.
> He descended into hell;
> the third day he rose again from the dead.
> He ascended into heaven,
> sits at the right hand of God,
> the Father Almighty;
> from thence he shall come
> to judge the living and the dead.
> I believe in the Holy Spirit,

the Holy Catholic Church,
the communion of saints,
the forgiveness of sins,
the resurrection of the body,
and life everlasting. Amen.

Act of Contrition

O my God, I am heartily sorry
for having offended you,
and I detest all my sins
because of your just punishments,
but most of all because they offend you, my God,
who are all good and deserving of all love.
I firmly resolve,
with the help of your grace,
to sin no more
and to avoid the occasions of sin. Amen.

The Doxology

Glory be to the Father,
and to the Son,
and to the Holy Spirit,
as it was in the beginning,
is now,
and ever shall be,
world without end. Amen.

Then add a prayer asking God to bless each member of the family. Conclude with the Sign of the Cross.

This is just one collection of prayers for the family. Each family has its own favorites that they may wish to add on. Some of these are as follows:

The Rosary

It can be prayed in the ordinary way of announcing the Mystery at the start of each decade. The Mysteries of the Rosary are:

Joyful Mysteries

The Annunciation
The Visitation
The Nativity
The Presentation
The Finding in the Temple

Sorrowful Mysteries

The Agony in the Garden
The Scourging
The Crowning with Thorns
The Carrying of the Cross
The Crucifixion

Glorious Mysteries

The Resurrection
The Ascension
The Descent of the Holy Spirit
The Assumption
The Crowning of Mary as Queen of Heaven

The Scriptural Rosary can also be prayer, perhaps praying just one decade of it a night. (Cf. *Scriptural Rosary,* published by the Christianica Center, 6 N. Michigan Avenue, Chicago, Ill. 60602.)

The Memorare

Remember, O most gracious Virgin Mary,
that never was it known
that anyone who fled to your protection,
implored your help,
or sought your intercession
was left unaided.
Inspired by this confidence, we fly unto you,

O Virgin of virgins, our Mother!
To you we come,
before you we stand, sinful and sorrowful.
O Mother of the Word Incarnate,
despise not our petitions,
but in your mercy hear and answer us. Amen.

The Prayer of St. Francis of Assisi

Lord, make me an instrument of thy peace.
Where there is hatred, let me sow love;
where there is injury, pardon;
where there is doubt, faith;
where there is despair, hope;
where there is darkness, light;
and where there is sadness, joy.
O Divine Master,
grant that I may not so much seek
to be consoled as to console;
to be understood, as to understand;
to be loved, as to love.
For it is in giving that we receive,
it is in pardoning that we are pardoned,
and it is in dying that we are born to eternal life.
Amen.

Prayer of St. Ignatius

Take, Lord, and receive all my liberty,
my memory, my understanding, and my entire will,
all that I have and possess.
You have given all to me.
To you, O Lord, I return it.
All is yours; dispose of it entirely according
to your will.
Give me your love and your grace,
for this is sufficient for me.

Group Prayer

Where two and three meet in my name,
I shall be there with them (Mt 18:20).

The first Christians met in their homes to pray. These meetings were characterized by joy and resulted in a generous sharing of their goods, "distributing them according to what each one needed" (Acts 2:45).

An exciting result of the post-Vatican II Church is that this is happening again. Good Christians are meeting in their homes to pray. I am finding that this is occurring with an increasing frequency and could very well become a ground swell out of which the spiritual renewal called for by Vatican II can further take place. They begin in various ways, usually started by one or two people eager for the support that group prayer brings, and develop by word of mouth rather than through any formal advertising.

I think group prayer can provide an extraordinary means of support for your private prayer and can be the catalyst that will enable us to realize that all prayer, after all, is group prayer. By this I mean that our private prayer ought never to be a selfish undertaking but ought to be for the community at large. Even when we are making private petitions the petitions when made to the Father of us all become a family thing, an affair that ought to concern us all as brothers and sisters. Group prayer makes available, in a tangible way, the lived experience of belonging to the Mystical Body and can be an enormous support for us who are eager to develop our personal prayer lives.

How did group prayer begin again to enter the Christian community? I don't know exactly, but I surmise that as ordinary Christians became reawakened to the value and importance of prayer and spirituality for their own Christian and human development, they also found that the organized and institutional Church was not responding to their needs and decided to do something about it. What they did was get together and pray, not in church, not even in the parish hall, but in their homes. This is happening with an increasing frequency now and is no doubt adding to a strengthening of the parish community, for all authentic prayer, in Jesus' name, ought to build community, not detract from it.

What does one do to find a prayer group? A good place to begin would be your local church. Ask whether there are any prayer groups meeting regularly and see whether you could join one. It would be helpful to ask what kind of prayer groups are meeting and not presume that they are all alike. They are not. For instance, there are groups that pray from Scripture with long pauses of silence in between the Scripture passages; others have a charismatic bent to them; still others see their prayer group as a place for faith sharing, and so on. Hence, it would be well to ask beforehand and then join the one that appeals to you the most. This may imply visiting several of them first before deciding on the one you are comfortable with. I think that must be your criterion for ultimately deciding on a particular group. When you have an at-home feeling about it, stay there. You have arrived!

But let us say there are no groups around. How does one start a prayer group? By inquiring among your friends, whom you know have similar desires, whether they would be willing to get together regularly to pray. You may be surprised at the response. For some reason people feel bashful about expressing their needs in this area, but, when asked, open up joyfully to the suggestion.

Then decide on a day and a time. Once a week, for one to one and a half hours, seems to be a fairly acceptable schedule. Once that is decided, it would be helpful to volunteer your own home for the first meeting, with the understanding that future meetings will be held in other members' homes—this so that no one person has the weekly responsibility of hosting it. Once this is all decided, plan the prayer itself. You may do the planning the first time, but I think it is helpful to take turns leading the prayer instead of expecting one person to lead it every week. Of course, it is possible to meet without a leader and trust that the Spirit will pray through the members, each in his or her own way. I have found, however, that frequently such a leaderless group becomes a soapbox for one or two more vocal members who take over the group and monopolize the prayer. This is not to say that leaderless groups cannot function effectively but it is to say that inherent temptations to power and glory exist in such a situation.

But if you decide to plan the prayer, do so simply and without anxiety. Remember that it is prayer you are planning and not a performance. Here are some guidelines. The planning could begin with switching off most of the lights and/or lighting a candle to remind all present that they are now entering sacred space. Then everyone can become silent and still. After some moments like this begin by using a prayer found in this book and expand it as the weeks go by to the many excellent prayer exercises contained in the books I have recommended, or use any others that you may be particularly attracted to. After an hour or so of prayer you may want to take a short break and then return to share with one another what you experienced in your prayer. In this I think it is very important that the prayer group not deteriorate into a soapbox for the prayer leader or any member of the group for that matter. Keep in mind that the point of the gathering is prayer, and let this point be expressed by each member through a sensitivity and hospitality toward all the other members. That means that no one should monopolize the sharing period. Speak only what comes out of your silence; then the Lord can be heard. Further, it is essential to feel quite free not to share verbally if that is where you are. Coercion ought never to be even implied in the sharing session. At the same time the value of sharing one's own intimate experiences of the Lord-within is not to be brushed off, for it can provide a source of encouragement to others who may feel that God is not quite that near, or is not quite that concerned.

Other than the implicit values of praying together there can also be explicit beneficial consequences. The more·we experience the love of the Lord in the group, and in one another, the more we become sensitized to the needs of the world around us. Consequently, it is possible that the prayer group members may eventually want to involve themselves in works of love, not only for one another but for those brothers and sisters less fortunate than themselves. In fact, an effective barometer of the success of the prayer group can be found here. Is the group becoming more loving, more concerned for one another as well as for others? Is the group becoming more concerned about such issues as poverty, injustice, war and human rights? Is the group choosing to become involved in any of these issues in a concrete way, or are they content to talk about it, and then not to respond to the need, whatever it may be? This is the gauge by which we determine the progress of the prayer group that gathers in Jesus' name.

Finally, I think it most important that new members be greeted with graciousness and hospitality. They must not be left alone or given any indication that they ought not to be there. Initially new members will feel a bit uncomfortable, as one would joining any new group, but it is up to the members of the prayer group to go out of their way to make their transition into the group as smooth and as loving as possible.

A book I would recommend for a prayer group is *Redemptive Intimacy* by Dick Westley (Twenty-Third Publications, P.O. Box 180, Mystic, Conn. 06355). Of

91

course the other books I have mentioned in this chapter can also be fine starting points for your adventure of praying as a Christian community of faith. I pray that you will find in your group the love and the support for your own prayer lives that I have found in mine.

3

Consequences of Prayer

Introduction

I have described some of the many ways to God that are available to us. Entering into a life of prayer through them can literally transform our lives so that we can boldly reassert our own uniqueness as daughters and sons of our Abba Father God. This uniqueness is made visible through two foundational elements of our humanity, freedom and love. Praying can result in these becoming functioning realities in our lives. Yet in the face of the many inimical forces that surround us, freedom and love can be difficult to realize in formal prayer alone without a broader appreciation of the Incarnation of Jesus.

The Incarnation of Jesus means that God became human. He entered fully into our condition and, through the life and teachings, the death and resurrection of his Son Jesus transformed our perspective of ourselves and the world we live in. No longer are we to look upon ourselves as worthless and unloved; rather, Jesus taught that if we believe in him:

> . . . my Father will love you;
> we shall come to you
> and make our home with you (Jn 14:23).

This means that our God dwells not only amongst us but within us as well. Leading a life of prayer enables us to recognize this humbling truth. It helps us see that God is readily available to us not only in our times of prayer and solitude but through one another as well. Hence, it is very important that we humbly acknowledge that our prayer lives extend outward to our brothers and sisters. This means that the redemptive power of God's love is not experienced in prayer alone but also through listening to the people in our lives and to the events of our days.

This becomes particularly necessary when we have trials and difficulties and we sense that prayer alone will not help us through them. This is very true. It won't. In the face of some calamities, resorting to formal prayer alone without taking advantage of the many other ways God speaks to us is inadequate. This is when it is very important to remember that God works through our brothers and sisters as well, and, acknowledging this, humbly reach out to them for help.

In this chapter I will describe some of these painful times. Often they are connected to the two foundational elements of our humanness—freedom and love. Hence, I will describe four places from which un-freedom can cause us pain and three places out of which love can be allayed. They are not exhaustive but are intended as pointers from which prayer, and the help of our brothers and sisters, can facilitate a new freedom and a return of love.

The four places of our un-freedoms I will describe are in family life, in religion, in politics and government, and in economics. The three places out of which love can be lost are in relationships, in loneliness, and in illness and death.

Dealing with these from a fuller appreciation of the incarnation in our lives can return us to our position of uniqueness as God's daughters and sons. Formal prayer combined with the help of our brothers and sisters can facilitate this process and so witness to this word the power of God's word, of peace and justice, and love.

Freedom

To be free is a yearning that we all have, yet few of us seem to be truly free. The world we live in appears to mitigate against our freedom, and often we may find ourselves struggling to assert our independence in the face of numerous forces, both personal and impersonal, that try to keep us in servitude. Our work, our family, even our religion seem to oppress us at times. The result is that our yearning for freedom remains just that. Yet Jesus called us to freedom. He said:

If you make my word your home,
you will indeed be my disciples.
You will learn the truth,
and the truth will make you free (Jn 8:31–32).

It is this freedom that can be a consequence of prayer, for in prayer we make Jesus' word our home, and in doing this we do learn the truth, and this truth will indeed set us free. What is this truth?

Above all, I believe, this truth is God's love for us in Jesus. In prayer we can experience this love, and as we do a freedom to be ourselves emerges. It is the freedom that comes from knowing that one is loved dearly, without any conditions attached to that love. When we know this, the inimical forces that threaten our freedom begin to be rendered powerless and we can resolutely face our un-freedoms with a new hope, a new courage. I will mention some of them here, trusting that by so "naming the demons" you may recognize them in yourself and allow your prayer to free you from them.

95

In Family Life

The first of these areas is in family life itself. Unlike perhaps any other time in history the family unit appears to be disintegrating. Untold anguish is being caused as a result of this. We find that the extended family is becoming increasingly a sociological phenomenon of the past. It is a rare family today that contains two or three generations living in one house. The stability and the familial continuity it afforded are hence no more. The often painfully necessary action of sending the aged to "old folks' homes" results in children growing up with only an intermittent sense of family continuity.

Then there is the break-up of the nuclear family itself. Divorces are today on a two to one ratio with marriages in their early years. Many of these marriages break up though only after one or two or even more children have been born into them. The reasons, of course, are many, and there is no intent here of "casting the first stone," but the fact remains that the stability that the nuclear family in the recent past enjoyed is no more.

This fact leads to the traumatic experiences our children have to endure in the earliest years of their lives. Even as they try to cope with the world around them, the very first anchors they have are no more. In their stead, the children can be faced with a bewildering number of new faces and personality types that they have to deal with in the new relationships which the parent with whom they are living may be having. This has to cause not only confusion but a sense of insecurity in them.

Hence we have a society that is becoming increasingly disconnected with its roots, a society in which the nuclear family unit is breaking up at an alarming rate, and a society with many confused and insecure children.

But it is not only the children who are insecure. They may be the ones to manifest it most obviously but they are not alone in their insecurities. By no means. The divorced father or mother likewise experiences insecurity, of a traumatic nature at times. Most understandably! The bottom has fallen out of their lives; the one they promised to love and support all of their days is no more. The message received of course from this is, "Then I must be no good." And how about the insecurity of the one doing the leaving? There is a sense of failure, and, of course, guilt. "I did all I could but she was destroying me, so I had to get out," and "If I stayed with him any longer I feel I would have become completely neutered," are fairly common explanations. But as convincing as these words may be, there is still the anger, and the guilt, and the shame, and the confusion that come with the sense of failure. Insecurity on a very fundamental level is the consequence.

This insecurity can lead to fear. And the fear can lead to a paralysis that can prevent the healing from beginning for a long time. In the fear is the un-freedom. There is a sense of being overwhelmed by inimical forces, be they "the other man or woman" or "the irreconcilable differences" or whatever. The world seems to be a very big place at such a time, and one may feel like a lost child in a dark forest of mysterious and threatening beings.

At a time like this prayer can be the quiet answer, though, depending on the severity of the condition, I don't believe that prayer alone is quite enough. Professional help can be an invaluable asset, as well as a shoulder or two to cry on. Prayer, though, can offer the still point that can become the inchoate place out of which the healing can begin. For, in prayer, one can find that all is not lost, but rather that the God-within is still there, as loving and as supportive and as forgiving as he ever was. Recognizing the affirmation he brings can enable the healing to begin. In companionship with him, drawing on the inner resource his presence provides, one can begin to face the world again with a new confidence and resoluteness that one may have not thought again possible. Prayer is also the tool that can prevent the break-up of families. It can be the bonding that cements the love together and prevents the disintegration from ever beginning. I feel this is most important for today's family, given the many pressures it is subjected to in the fast-paced, seductive, modern world. A family that prays is a family that stays open to God, and that means staying open to one another. The freedom this results in will be the freedom of God's own daughters and sons.

In Religion

The second area out of which our un-freedoms derive may initially sound surprising. This is because traditionally it has been taught as the source of freedom. Yet today many are finding that it too shackles and can be a quite oppressive factor in our lives. This is the area of religion.

Perhaps it would be helpful to first explain the word "religion." For some years I taught a course on "World Religions" to college students. In the introductory lectures we dealt with the beginnings of religion. It was most interesting to note the incredulity on the part of some students when confronted with the origins of religion. In essence religion originated out of the fears and anxieties, the awe and the intimidations that the environment produced. When our ancestors began to believe that somehow they had to appease these natural forces, and organized their appeasement around a set of rules and regulations, we had religion. The incredulity of the students stemmed from the fact that many of them saw modern religions doing the same thing. It is true that contemporary religion's appeasements are not as crass as our primitive ancestors' appeasements were but, nevertheless, appeasement of a fear-inspiring God appears to be at the bottom of much of our modern day religious sensibilities as well. And the arguments in their favor seem just as convincing as were the arguments of our ancestors, when sacrificing a young virgin, for example, was seen as imperative if a drought were to be ended, or a rich crop harvested.

Yet, the Judaeo-Christian God, through his prophets and the leaders of his people, and indeed through his only Son, Jesus, shouted time and time again from many a proverbial mountaintop that this was not what he wanted. Not this at all! For example, through the oracle of Micah he proclaims that it is not sacrifice of appeasement that he wants; rather he indignantly repeats:

> What is good has been explained to you. This is what Yahweh asks of you: only this, to act justly, to love tenderly, and to walk humbly with your God (Mi 6:8).

Then again we have Jesus clearly calling us to the great commandment:

> You must love the Lord your God with all your heart, with all your soul, with all your strength, and with all your mind, and your neighbor as yourself (Lk 10:27).

This is what we are to be about—only this.

Yet organized religion offers us frequently a God that is impossible to so love. How can one be expected to love a God that quite apart from not being on our side appears all too often to be against us, waiting with hand poised in mid-air, as it were, to strike us down? And for what? For not following the rules and laws of institutions that operate in his name and mete out punishments in his name for its recalcitrant members. The institutions of religion, consequently, delimit God's availability by specifying certain "approved" channels of his love and, as a result, control and limit the freedom of its members. Institutions in this world use people to get things, usually the "things" of self-perpetuation and profit. Religious institutions appear often to be no different. This may not be the actual case, or the initial intent of religious institutions, but many find this to be the case, hence giving God a bad name. So those who turn to religion do not find there a place of freedom but all too frequently experience it as a place of imprisonment. Consequently religion is seen as yet another oppressor and anything but a liberator.

Freedom from religious oppression can occur if one begins a life of prayer. In prayer one encounters God devoid of the trappings of religious dressing. For in that quiet encounter we meet a gentle, caring, non-judgmental friend who invites us to a shameless intimacy with him. The more we listen to our heart—and remember "heart" includes all that is non-corporeal about us—the more we find a place of true freedom and caring love. In our place of solitude we can find freedom if we but choose to believe that the God-within truly dwells there. This is how liberation can be at hand. To believe. To make the effort of the will that faith calls for, and say, "Yes, I do believe God loves me. I am not alone; he really wants to live in me and be my constant companion. I will reach out to him and let him free me from my fears, and return to believing in him." It is through encountering the love of God in prayer that we can encounter the love of God in church. For ought not our institutionalized worship be the climactic and communal expression of our personal faith lived out in prayer? The more we pray, therefore, the more we can offer the challenge for authentic conversion to our institutional Church's leaders, and so together build up a community of love in God's name on this earth.

Here again, though, as in the stresses found in contemporary family life, prayer alone is not enough. Gone are the days when the person in the pew is only a spectator. Leaving the running of religion to those in leadership in the churches is no longer an adequate response. For everyone who is baptized has an obligation to serve the kingdom of God; we see more and more religious and lay men and women are recognizing this, and more importantly doing something about it. Today, unlike the last few centuries, there are numerous opportunities for lay people and non-ordained religious to become leaders in the churches. It is time that more advantage was taken of these opportunities. The permanent diaconate has been reinstituted; the new offices of eucharistic ministers, lectors, liturgists, and directors of religious education have opened up, offering many new ways for the non-clerical baptized person to serve. The natural opposition on the part of some clerics to these new ministries for lay persons and for religious is understandable; they feel threatened and intimidated by them. For those who have found their self-worth and identity in their function as priest or minister, these new opportunities appear as an infringement on their territoriality. They are to be understood and not condemned, treated with compassion and love, and not judged. However, they must also learn the truth that all of us have a part to play in spreading the Kingdom of God. It is not a task reserved for the hierarchical leaders of the Church alone; we all share in it. If we can realize this, and work together, then the love of God can the sooner become evident on this earth.

This task can only be done if we lead lives of prayer. This is because in prayer we encounter the truth. We find it in the promptings of the God-within that will enable us, the disciples of the future, to step out and be counted as leaders of a Church steeped in faith and love. And that future is today for all of us who want to transform the institutions of religion into pillars of faith.

In Politics and Government

The third area out of which we may feel helpless and shackled, and which could provide a focus for our developing prayer life, is the area of politics and government. We live in a time both of unparalleled freedom and equally unparalleled oppression. The democracies, on the one hand, promise and give us considerable freedom of thought and action, while the totalitarian regimes seek to govern through domination. Both forms of government have groups resisting them at various points in their operation, and frequently these resistances are quelled either through violent military intervention or less violent judicial means. Regardless of the particular point of the resistance, it seems evident that a loss of freedom, of some kind or another, is what is being resisted. An example from a very current issue is that of nuclear war. Other current issues are the crisis in Poland, and of course the ongoing conflicts in the Middle East. A relative newcomer to the scene is Central America and the resistance to the oppressive regimes operating there.

The fears these generate are very real. The "communist threat" is not to be ignored. The anxiety over totalitarian regimes seeking to dominate not only their own citizens but their neighbors as well is no light matter, but the average person, as much as he or she may want to, feels helpless in the face of such monumental problems. Trying to effect changes in government through the electoral system, or perhaps writing an occasional letter to a representative in government, seems a puny and largely ineffectual way of expressing one's fears and anxieties. Now one who is praying and becoming more attuned to life's potential goodness may feel even more helpless and frustrated than one who is not. The contradiction, between the private experiences of God's intimate love with its resulting joys and freedoms and the sorrows and struggles of "the real world," can lead one to doubt God's power to save. But this doubt can be healthy, for it can stimulate the question: "What can I do? How do I help transform the world I live in, from one filled with power and fear and hatred to one of love and compassion?"

The answer is to be found, I believe, in allowing the God-within, specifically in the life of his Son Jesus, to teach us his way. How did Jesus act and behave when he was on this earth, and, incidentally, living under an oppressive foreign regime? How did Jesus deal with injustice? What did he do with his enemies, who were certainly no pushovers but rather the religio-political leaders of the time? I believe that the answer to our questions can be found here, and it is out of these answers that a legitimate Christian response to the oppressive actions of politics and government are to be found.

Jesus taught love of enemies. He also instructed us to do good to those who hate us, to bless those who curse us and to pray for those who treat us badly. This is nothing less than a practical living out of the great twofold commandment to love God and to love our neighbor as ourselves. It is hence central to Jesus' teaching. The earliest Christians, those closest to Jesus in his earthly life and ministry, sought to live out this command during a time when being a Christian was a most dangerous thing to be. Persecutions were many, crucifixions and brutal torture of Christians were commonplace, especially under the emperor Nero, and oppression under a totalitarian regime was the order of the day.

How did the earliest Christians respond to all of this? It is perhaps well known that Christians in the early Church were avowed pacifists—in fact one of the reasons they were persecuted was that they refused to be conscripted into the Roman army. But they were anything but passive! Pacifism didn't mean refusing to stand up to oppression; rather it meant refusing to use physical force and military might to attain its end. There are many instances of Christians resisting oppressive and unjust laws and decrees, resisting not with physical violence but rather with an active and fearless non-cooperation with Roman laws that contradicted Christian conscience. For example, John Cadoux, in his book *The Early Church and the World,* writes as follows:

> One Christian tore down the first edict of persecution posted up by Diocletianus; another fearlessly seized the governor's hand as he was in the act of sacrificing and exhorted him to abandon his error; another strode forward in open court and rebuked the judge for his ruthless sentences. A Christian woman dragged to the altar, and commanded to sacrifice upon it, kicked it over (as quoted in"Fighting Fire with Water" by Richard Taylor and Ronald Sider in *Sojourners,* April 1983).

Hence early Christians were anything but passive in the way they resisted oppression and injustice. For them the teachings of Jesus on love of enemies did not at all contradict resisting their unjust proclamations and laws. In fact, refusing to resist them would have been far worse, for that would be tantamount to approving their behavior and hence approving not the Kingdom of love and justice that Jesus proclaimed but rather the very opposite, the forces of evil, the forces of Satan.

It is very clear that Jesus himself set up this practical response to his own command to love God and neighbor, first by driving out the money changers from the temple together with all the abuses of the temple they symbolized. As is said in the Gospel of Luke:

> According to scripture, he said "my house will be a house of prayer. But you have turned it into a robbers' den" (Lk 19:46).

Then again in his own interrogation before the high priest he hardly took their questions lying down. He stood up to the questioning of the high priest, and when one of the guards slapped him for "talking back" to the high priest, Jesus replied:

> If there is something wrong in what I said, point it out;
> but if there is no offense in it, why do you strike me?"
> (Jn 18:23).

His entire ministry, in fact, was centered around standing up for the truth for as he also said:

> If you make my word your home you will indeed be
> my disciples; you will learn the truth and the truth will
> make you free (Jn 8:31–32).

I have noted earlier that one of the most appealing descriptions of this "truth" that I have heard is that truth is God's desire to enter into an intimate relationship with us, and so free us from all that binds us. For once one encounters the true love of God and allows oneself to enter into that loving union, freedom from the powers of this world can naturally follow. How? By experiencing true love. It gives us the security and the stability we need to boldly stand up to injustice and oppression. It gives us the confidence we need to act for justice and equality, for the freedom that all of us are called to as daughters and sons of the one Father. This, of course, occurs in prayer. As we encounter God's truth there develops in us a longing to stamp out the lies of this world. Most understandably! The lies of this world have been most convincingly peddled by most of the leaders of this world, whose public institutions claim to govern peoples but instead oppress them. When we experience what God's rule is like, false leadership stands out in sharp relief.

In prayer, through discovering and experiencing the immense love God has for us, we are given the courage to stand up to the lies and take the consequences of doing so with an equanimity rivaling the psalm-singing of the early martyrs as they were led out to become food for the lions of the Roman arenas.

What can happen to us today if we allow a cry for justice to become evident? Probably the same thing that happened to Jesus: crucifixion. But if we are truly people of prayer, as Jesus was, we will find strength in the persecution through "the truth" that will be alive in our hearts. Armed with that we can endure the torments of this world with a deeply experienced peace, for the torments will not lead to ultimate death but rather, as in Jesus' own crucifixion, to a resurrection of abundant life.

What does this imply on a practical level? I think it is an important question, for it brings the redemptive mystery down to our own hearths and homes—where it belonged in the first place anyway! It implies that we cannot just sit back and allow injustice and oppression to occur; we must inform ourselves and others we meet of their occurrence. We can participate in groups that peacefully resist oppressive structures; we can write letters of protest to people in power expressing our Christian views; we can form little organizations in our own neighborhoods to better educate and inform ourselves of what is going on, and the like. What is clear though is that if we experience God's love for us in prayer we will feel compelled to go forth and share his love with others; and often this can be done by going forth

> . . . to bring good news to the poor,
> to bind up hearts that are broken;
> to proclaim liberty to captives,
> freedom to those in prison . . .
> to comfort all those who mourn and

to give them for ashes a garland (Is 61:1–3).

Out of this we can gradually begin to discover with greater insight the truth that lies in freedom, and from this discovery boldly proclaim it to the entire world. Then our life of prayer will unshackle not only us but all we meet with the joy that it brings, the freedom it initiates.

In Economics

The fourth area that may shackle us, and hence be a specific point for our prayer life to lead us into a new freedom, is the area of economics. Many people around the world today have as their prime preoccupation the state of the economy. Making ends meet, finding enough money to make the next car or house payment, engaging in "deficit spending," or worrying about being "laid off" or just finding oneself without a job at all—these are serious matters that affect all of us and tend to facilitate a sense of helplessness that in turn can make us feel dehumanized, or, worse still, irrelevant in an unfeeling economic index. How can a life of prayer help us here? One may initially entertain a justifiable skepticism as to prayer's efficacy in this so "worldly and secular" area, and wonder if this may be stretching the value of prayer a bit too far. This skepticism emerges out of a too pragmatic approach to solutions. Prayer is not magic; the state of the economy is hence not going to be transformed to our advantage if we develop a life of prayer. But what a life of prayer can do is transform those involved in the economy, and that in turn can have far-reaching results not only for the world at large but for ourselves as well. What prayer can offer us is the freedom that comes from a totally new perspective about the economy, so much so that regardless of the financial straits we may find ourselves in we cease to be dominated by it, and instead find in the intimate companionship with the God-within a resource that can make our sometimes meager economic resources appear sufficient indeed. For love develops a truer perspective on our life and the world we live in. It invites us to implement the teaching of Jesus:

> But you, you must not set your hearts on things to eat and things to drink; nor must you worry. It is the pagans of this world who set their hearts on all these things. Your Father well knows you need them. No; set your hearts on his kingdom, and these other things will be given you as well. There is no need to be afraid, little flock, for it has pleased your Father to give you the kingdom (Lk 12:29–32).

Once I knew of an old lady, the wife of a sharecropper, who had led a life of constant prayer. She was now almost destitute, had lived alone since her husband's premature death, and was in failing health. Yet she was a memorable example of the perspective that prayer can provide upon one's economic state. Her constant refrain was how good God was, how fortunate her life had been, with a loving husband, and children who had given her little trouble as they grew up. "God will provide," she would say, when dipping into her almost empty "bank drawer." She would find so little in there that her next meal seemed to be an uncertain thing. But the amazing thing was that God always did provide. She never went hungry; she always would get enough money to fix another meal. And that was not all. At her age, and in the economic straits she was in, one would expect her to be preoccupied with making ends meet. Not at all! That would be farthest from the truth. Hers was a busy life. She would be constantly busy caring "for the poor and sick," as she would say. She would run errands for them, pick up their mail from the rural post office and deliver it to them, work in all the charitable functions at church and help raise money for the poor, and generally be a most loving neighbor to all. Hers was a busy life indeed, and rare were the times she would complain except when her arthritis got the better of her, which "kept her from helping peoples," she would say. Actually, there was much more wrong with her than her arthritis, but her other ailments she didn't complain about, so one would never know. In the midst of her busy life and economic destitution she was happy. Spending time with her always cheered my heart and forced a new perspective on me in a way that was refreshing and challenging. For what she exemplified was Christ's injunction not to worry about clothing, and food, and drink but rather to set one's heart on his Kingdom, and "these things will be given you as well" (Lk 12:29–31). The truth of the matter was that these words were fulfilled for her daily. Somehow, in some way, she would find the money to live, and to live contendedly. People who knew her were surprised at how well she did; she never was. She took it for granted, and with a chuckle that lit up her whole face would say simply, "God does provide!"

Most of us, however, have not attained the freedom that she evidently had. Life reveals itself as a continuing struggle to make ends meet, and when the ends are met new and more expensive items are purchased so that the quality of our lives can be improved, leading to yet another struggle to make these new ends meet, and so on. Now there is nothing wrong with seeking an improved life-style, but there is definitely something wrong when one becomes preoccupied with it to the exclusion of more spiritual and hence uniquely human matters. It is a question of perspective. It is also a question of freedom. One of the prime ways that our freedom can become curtailed is found here. When the thrust of our lives becomes so centered on material gain and fluctuations of the economic indices that we become controlled and shackled by them, we are not free. We start worrying, and allow anxiety to rule our lives. We begin to lose perspective.

There is another dehumanizing consequence, in the quest for economic gain for its own sake, that can affect us. It is the quest for power. Within all of us there is the temptation to become powerful. One of the quickest ways of realizing that aim is economic dominance attained through the acquisition of wealth. Once we have wealth we also have power, and rare indeed is the person who will not give in to the temptation to wield that power, either through manipulating people less powerful, or controlling events to suit his or her own situation. This person soon begins to identify his or her self worth with the "things" he or she possesses and not with the unique and profound relationship of love to which the God-within keeps inviting the person. Hence, this person begins to deal not with the truth that is this ennobling relationship of love but rather with the lies that the false security of wealth and power so easily provides. This false security makes such a person insensitive to the potential for the joy that "surpasses all understanding," within him or her, usually consequenting itself in cruelty and intolerance. Such a person looks upon prayer and the quest for a loving union with God as something that belongs to weaklings and economic underlings who have nothing better to do. It is not the work of "real people" who have to make a successful go of it in this world! The pride that all of this breeds becomes well ensconced in that person's psyche, and it is hard indeed for such a person to break out of the bonds that shackle him or her. I think these results of economic wealth are what prompted Jesus to observe:

> How hard it is for those who have riches to make their way into the kingdom of God! Yes, it is easier for a camel to pass through the eye of a needle than for a

rich man [or woman] to enter the kingdom of God (Lk
18:24–25).

Yet, I know of many wealthy people who have not
succumbed to these temptations. To a person, I find they
are people of prayer. Wealthy they are, but through developing an intimate, loving union with the God-within, they
are not controlled by their wealth. They exemplify the
words of Jesus:

Where your treasure is there will be your heart also (Lk
12:34).

Their treasure is not in their wealth but in the knowledge that they are dearly loved by a God who yearns constantly for an ever more intimate union with them. They
can be easily detected through the love, the generosity,
and the humility with which they deal with their neighbors. They don't lord it over anybody, they are not arrogant and pompous, but rather they see all people with the
eyes of God, with eyes that see in the less economically
fortunate not people to be dominated and manipulated
but rather brothers and sisters of the one Father in heaven.
Still, what of those whose wealth and power have
blinded them to the truth? I think there is little that can
be done if they are not open to conversion, to a willingness to admit their need of healing and of love. The most
one can do is trust in God working in their lives, and
intercede for them in prayer, believing that God can break
through even the strongest suit of armor. As a part of this
prayer I believe that there is also a responsibility on the
part of those nearest to them to challenge and occasionally confront them with love but also with firmness. Prayer
alone here is not enough. One is also called to reach out
to the powerful and the arrogant and try to touch them
with the power of God's love that can be so freeing. It is

not easy, but it can be done if one knows in prayer that one is not alone in the attempt but that within our hearts as well dwells One who invites and longs for an intimacy with the wealthy and powerful as well as with the poor.

Challenging the rich and powerful has its dangers. The first of these is an almost unconscious exoneration of ourselves from having anything to do with their wealth. While it may be true that we may not be wealthy, the attitude we have toward others less fortunate than ourselves could well include us among the rich. Wealth here is not to be seen as just having a lot of money but rather as a stance that makes us self-righteous.

A second danger is seeing ourselves as crusaders standing up for what is right, battling the injustices of society, fighting against the exploitation of the poor and so on, and failing to recognize that in our own lives we are being unjust and oppressive. It is easier to join a cause and fight injustice in the abstract than to tackle problems of resentment, intolerence, and coldness in our personal relationships. I believe we have to begin with ourselves and through the example of our lives proclaim the Kingdom of God's justice and love on this earth.

A third danger is limiting our understanding of the evils of economic domination. Jesus preached a radical equality of all people, and a practical consequence of responding to him is working for an equal distribution of resources. It is not enough to encourage the rich to be generous to the poor. We must recognize our radical connectedness with each other. This is the importance of belonging to the one body of Christ: that at the core of our being we are all brothers and sisters of the one Father. It is from this prayed-through realization that economic justice and social justice can be made into reality.

I have tried to mention four areas out of which unfreedom in our lives can evolve, trusting that as they are surfaced one may find places from which one's prayer life can lead into a new freedom out of the experiential encounter with the God-within. They were the area of family life, the area of religion, the area of politics and government, and finally the area contained in the economic sphere.

These are, of course, only four areas. There are many others; each of us has to identify our particular area of unfreedom for ourselves. Regardless of the starting point, entering an experience of unconditional love can offer us a liberation that can free us to be that loving human being that we so long to be.

Love

The point of this book is realized when one chooses to experience one's own lovableness through prayer, and when, out of that experience, one becomes a more sensitive, caring, empowered human being than before. The sophisticated, technologically advancing world of today can be rehumanized only if we develop, to a far greater strength than ever before, this capacity we have for love.

I am trying to challenge us to discover anew the means we have to regain our humanity in the face of an impersonal and inimical world. We do this by first developing our capacity for reflection through prayer, and out of that power regaining the freedoms to be fully human that we may have lost. The final consequence of this process is regaining our appreciation of ourselves and of the people we live with and work with through an authentic, Christ-initiated love.

Love is the critical factor of differentiation between animals and ourselves. It is, more than any other emotion, that which makes us human. Yet it is a word greatly misunderstood. It has been cheapened so much, peddled by so many, and used as the sales gimmick in so many places that the word's meaning and power has long since been obfuscated. Yet the quest for it is a full-time occupation for many. What "it" is, though, varies in meaning from person to person. No one definition suffices; no one experience can ever articulate it adequately. Love has more "experts" describing it than probably any other "commodity." It is the Goliath of the sales business in that in its name just about anything can be sold, from the preparation that relieves the big H (hemorrhoids) to the "shimmering island in the sun vacation" that promises to relieve everything else! And in spite of recurring disillusionment the sales continue to mount, the tantalizing promise of "love" continues to charm the buyers, and "love" as the hook that increases profits continues its dazzlingly successful career.

But is the capacity for authentic love in us increased by all this? Are our fondest yearnings to be a truly lovable person realized? I think not. The increasingly frenetic buying pace that some engage in borders more on desperation than satisfaction. There is, at the end of the shopping spree, the recognition of an emptiness that the purchase of all the clothes and goods in the world couldn't satisfy. One may detect, at such a moment, a sense of depression or futility, a feeling that in spite of all one's efforts, the love sought, the affirmation longed for, is not to be forthcoming. No matter how splendid the newly-purchased gown, the well-appointed jewelry, a feeling of dissatisfaction prevails, and quite apart from feeling lovable the reverse is often the result. The increasingly desperate hope that some entertain, to be affirmed and loved by another or others, seldom if ever gets realized through external allurements; in fact, the opposite is true, and all that is elicited is pity.

For love to blossom in our lives we must see it for what it is. We must understand that love presumes great selflessness and calls for a continuing commitment to the beloved. It is a process, not an event. And we must be will-

114

ing to engage in the discipline that this process demands. Love, like all gifts of immense value, is something that wishful thinking alone won't realize. It takes hard work and it demands perseverance. It is not for the immature or the selfish; it belongs to those who are willing to give of themselves without counting the cost, to those who think first of the other and then of themselves.

If one enters a life of prayer one is entering into this process of authentic love-making. As one disciplines oneself regularly in solitude and in an active listening to one's "heart," one will find a gentle voice within that persistently insists on one's lovableness regardless of what one may have done or not done, regardless of the opinions of the world one lives in that may say the opposite, that one is unworthy and unlovable. In prayer we will encounter an amazing inner voice that affirms us just as we are, no matter what we may think of ourselves. Slowly, as we listen more and more to this voice of Truth, we will come to appreciate ourselves to such an extent that the opinions of the world cease to have the impact they had before. And as this appreciation deepens we will be able to reach out to the brother or sister in our midst who needs healing, or companionship, or empathy. We will develop a genuineness that can eventually melt all the caustic remarks, the unfeeling observations, the veiled threats and cruel jokes, through bold and thoughtful replies that will neutralize the thoughtless, sensitize the arrogant.

The recognition of our own lovableness, and the resulting selfless loving of our brother and sister, is not an easy thing to do. Many are the emotions and events in our lives that mitigate against it. As much as we may pray, discipline ourselves, and find the solitude to hear the voice of Love within us, there are times when we just don't hear it at all. Then, in spite of all our good intentions, we find love slipping away, we find our ears going deaf to its quiet affirming of us. I will try to touch on three of these areas here in the hope that their perception can be altered, from being areas out of which love is deadened to areas out of which greater love can become possible. They are the area of human relationships, the area of loneliness, and the area of illness and death.

In Relationships

Unlike perhaps any other time in history a revolution is underway in human relationships. Old stereotypes are rapidly declining as permanent norms for relating to one another, and this is especially true in the area of human sexuality. The traditional roles that men were called to play are being seriously challenged by the liberation of women from a subservient position to equal partnership in the relationship. This is causing uncertainty and insecurity on the part of many men and women, and the ensuing ambiguity can frequently leave one feeling helpless and intimidated. In this gathering storm love tends to be an uncertain anchor.

It is difficult to enter into solitude and try to develop our potential for love if the one closest to us appears to be denigrating it at the same time. This does not have to be overt but can simply be a result of the socio-cultural situation of the contemporary world. For example, if the wife in a love relationship is more successful in her profession, or if the husband has suffered a setback in his, the consequence can be quite threatening for both. The unspoken assumption is often made that because of the professional setback the traditional role of the husband is to be questioned and challenged. This can lead to arguments, misunderstandings and angry outbursts. These, of course, further erode the relationship, with some sort of a separation looming in the not too distant horizon, and love appears to be a remote and distant dream.

116

Then there is the contemporary phenomenon of increased mobility. It is now possible for wives as well as husbands to travel places far and near with considerable independence. If a relationship is not grounded solidly in trust, this can lead to problems for both. Suspicion about the behavior of the spouse or lover when away causes considerable stress and can lead to much turmoil. This process in itself can easily lead to a breakdown in the relationship.

Third, we have the proliferation of stories in the mass media of couple after couple breaking up over various issues, providing apparently easy societal approval for separation as a legitimate way out of a dilemma. This is not to say that separation is not the solution—in many cases it could be the most humanizing thing to do—but rather that the removal of the stigma obviates the necessity of working out the problems as in earlier times was thought necessary. The consequence is a terrible state of rejection and even despair, resulting in a pervading sense of personal failure and self-hatred. At times like this, prayer and solitude are the last things one wants, for the sense of alienation makes one feel that the God-within is away, and certainly not available for support and consolation. This, of course, is augmented by the enormous sense of guilt one feels, and difficult indeed is the struggle to believe that one is truly loved just as one is, in one's state of brokenness and despair.

How can a life of prayer penetrate such a veil of anguish? I don't think it can. Not on its own anyway. It seems that solitude alone, exerting oneself to hear the voice of God-within, cannot be done alone. I believe he is within at these times, but one needs help and support to hear him through the pain. The traditional advice of the minister or priest, to "go and pray about it," is a most inadequate and unresponsive answer to what is often a complex situation. This is not to say one ought not to pray. Not at all. However, it seems that the veil of anguish could be so thick that our attempts to allow God access into our woundedness needs support and help.

Talking to a friend, a spiritual director, or a compassionate professional could go a long way in piercing the veil and allowing the healing to begin. The prayer that heals here is the prayer that occurs when one human being reaches out to his or her wounded neighbor in love, and in that reaching out renders visible the compassion of God in a way that praying alone cannot facilitate.

Then what can begin to happen is true perspective. As one prays, believing that God is present though not tangibly felt, as one talks out one's pain, the realization returns that one is not alone, that one is supported and affirmed, and all is not lost. Out of the ashes of defeat and rejection there can arise a new sense of self-worth and purpose that can reveal inner resources that previously were unrecognized and hence unavailable for use.

A life of prayer can facilitate this process. If one has been praying, when the crisis strikes one has already the experience of love to fall back on and so has a greater sense of being loved and supported in the crisis. The perspective of one's own worth is hence not as easily lost, and one can, with a greater ease, regain one's self-confidence and self-respect.

It is natural, at a time of crisis, to seek a way out of it. Jesus, in Gethsemane, prayed, "Father, if you are willing, take this cup away from me." Yet central to the entire redemptive mystery of God's love for us is the cross. Surrendering to it, in complete faith that the Father is not going to do us in, brings forth the new life that is resurrection. This is not easy to do, of course, but if we know how very much the Father loves us, if we have experienced this love in prayer, then we can say with Jesus, "Nevertheless, let your will be done, not mine." It is not possible for us to say this if we have not been experientially aware of the Father's love before the crisis. Even if we have been, we cannot do it alone. Knowing this, the Father sent a friend to Jesus to give him the strength he needed to make it through that anguished night, for it is written:

An angel appeared to him,
coming from heaven to give him strength (Lk 22:43).

We are called to be that angel to people in anguish. We are called to support them and give them strength to believe that the God of love and of all consolation will not do them in, that it is not from escaping the anguish but by surrendering completely to it that peace and new life comes. For if we believe that God will bring greater life out of the death of failure and rejection, then we can endure and discover an amazing inner strength in the process that will make resurrection possible.

Often it is out of an anguish-filled experience of rejection in a relationship that one can develop a whole new way of thinking and feeling. One who surrenders to it and grows out of the suffering is a changed person. No longer does he or she feel isolated and alone, but rather a new sensitivity and awareness of the sufferings of others emerges. This is a person who, having endured the loss of love and experienced—through a counselor or spiritual director, as well as through prayer—the supportive loving inner voice of God, is one who can feel a greater empathy for his or her neighbor, but not only for one's neighbor. There will be a new appreciation for life, for the beauty of a flower and the magnificence of a Grand Canyon. There will be a renewed sense of hope and an attitude that affirms all living things, for now one knows of the power of the Spirit of Love that encourages new life to emerge out of the depths of despair and hopelessness. In this new recognition the old doubts as to one's lovableness and worthiness becomes transformed into a far deeper appreciation of self. Out of this new appreciation loving one's less fortunate brother or sister can flow with an easy naturalness and a greater sense of understanding than ever before. We will then become agents of true compassion and love facilitating the rehumanizing process that can melt all the guns and heal the fractures that this complex and rapidly changing world inflicts on us.

In Loneliness

The second area that can deaden us to our own lovableness is the malady that in its scope and range is reaching unparalleled lengths in the modern world. This is the area of loneliness. Unlike any other time in history we are living in a lonely world, a world in which automation and electronic conveniences, big corporations and unfeeling "service" institutions have caused a dislocation in many people between who they are and who they think they ought to be. The pressures of combating impersonal and often overpowering forces have caused a psychic breakdown that manifests itself in several maladjustive ways. Let me briefly surface four fairly common manifestations of this break-up. They are fear, aggression, a sense of inferiority, and an unfounded suspicion of everybody and everything.

Fear is a valid emotion. If someone is coming at me wieiding an axe, I would be very abnormal if I didn't get afraid. If I went to the doctor for tests and he told me I had an incurable disease I would feel some fear. Fear of things inimical to my well-being is normal; without fear we could end up doing dumb things that could cause our premature death! Fear is then a very necessary emotion, but when fear becomes exaggerated and irrational there is the possibility that we are using the fear to cover something else. One such feeling that an exaggerated fear covers is loneliness.

The fear of loneliness is becoming increasingly commonplace today. The society we live in fosters it, for genuine communication with another human being is fast becoming a rare activity. Apartment living in isolated units, subway and other mass transportation systems, the fast pace of the business world we live in, all cause us to become afraid that in the final analysis there is no one there. Indeed this is sadly the case for many. In fact, there is no one there. After joining so many clubs, after sitting in so many singles bars, after trying time after time to connect with another lonely person, one fears the bottom line is that one is alone. Fear can cover up loneliness. Efforts to deny the loneliness eventually prove ineffectual.

Another way of covering up loneliness is aggression. When one feels neglected, unloved, or unwanted, aggressive behavior emerges. This can be manifested through hostility, acts of dominance and manipulating others. This causes an intensification of the very isolation one seeks to alleviate. It is a way of punishing the world for one's feelings of isolation and loneliness. There are people who do not know how to humbly admit their need for love and companionship. They cannot see that their aggressive behavior is a defense against a world that appears uncaring and unloving. This makes them blind to their own worth and lovableness and compels them to find self-respect in acts of dominance and control. The loneliness is not lessened by it at all, and in a moment of fleeting honesty they may recognize this. Unfortunately, the way it is all too frequently handled is by an increase in the aggressive behavior, further alienating them from love and companionship. And so they find themselves at the top, but quite alone.

Feelings of inferiority are another way of covering up loneliness. One experiences great pain and anguish over remarks that are taken very personally and always inflict a sense of self-depreciation. One begins to feel inferior to everybody, and every situation is perceived as "too big to handle." There is a pervading sense of unworthiness coupled with a sense of shame that eventually can make the person lose his or her own individuality. This can be a tyrannical state to be in, for there seems to be no way out. And in its self-depreciation it prevents those who try to reach out and love the person from entering into their loneliness. It perpetuates itself, consequently allowing a paralysis to set in.

A final way in which loneliness manifests itself is through suspicion of everyone and everything. This is the person who can never find good in anything, who can take the warmest story of love and twist it into something evil. If anyone were to point that out, however, this person would feel greatly hurt and misunderstood. Further, he or she can find insults and self-deprecatory remarks in comments not even directed at him or her. There is a sense of pervading failure in all that he or she does. Frequently there is actual failure, for they are constantly trying to accomplish more than they are actually capable of doing. This person usually manipulates others, causing further alienation and loneliness. The suspicious can usually end up in either "taking up a noble cause" such as fighting for justice or battling a government policy, or else just giving up and withdrawing into a moodiness and general state of isolation and hopelessness. The end result consequently is an even greater sense of unlovableness and alienation.

These are some of the ways loneliness is dealt with. None of them work, and in fact the last state is usually worse than the first. The loneliness is intensified and any hope for love entering into their lives becomes lost. The search for love through all these maladjustive behaviors proves futile.

The eventual realization of this can be a very frightening thing indeed, unless one recognizes that these modus operandi for alleviating loneliness are quite simply wrong. Instead of questing for companionship and affirmation in all the wrong places and adopting maladjustive behaviors, the locus of our hope needs to be shifted, from without to within.

In the early years of Christianity there were many who sought God and a corresponding meaning to their existence by deliberately going off into the desert, there to live a solitary life as hermits. They sought intentionally what so many of us have thrust upon us. In their aloneness they found not loneliness but a rich and fulfilling companionship in the God-within that enabled them to become great lovers and empathizers. Throughout the ages—and certainly not in Christianity alone—there have been such people. They have become the great voices that have called us out of our busy and lonely lives to a different experience of fulfilling love that the crowded world fails to provide. In their aloneness they found love. By leading lives of quiet listening and gentle prayer they came to discover the intimate love of the God-within. That love brought them so much contentment and joy that loneliness was rarely a problem in their isolation.

Discovering the constant Companion of our hearts can alleviate our loneliness and give a richness to our lives that no contrived activity can provide. This is because in solitude we find the rich experience of a companioned aloneness in which the truth about ourselves is revealed: that we are loved intimately by God himself. In this place loneliness has no place, for here we let go of our anxieties without fear, our pretensions without anxiety. We do not have to prove ourselves or display any prowess or skill, for here, as we choose to convert our loneliness into solitude, we are in the presence of authentic love and genuine acceptance.

To transform the frightening sense of alienation that loneliness produces we need first to embrace it, admit that we are indeed lonely, admit that we are fearful of being abandoned, and then surrender to it in faith. We begin to believe that if we but cease our frenetic search for companionship and relax in the quiet acceptance of our condition, we will discover the condition transformed, finding a companion in the transformation who can radically change our perspective from that of an inward-looking, fear-filled person to one filled with an exuding joy. In a surprisingly short time we can drive away all our fears by discovering friends we previously saw only as threatening strangers, companions we previously viewed as only disinterested passersby. For once we choose to discover the love within we begin to see that loneliness is an unnecessary anxiety, and we can experience a liberation that mobilizes our paralyzing fears. Soon, knowing now that our support and strength comes from within in the presence of God himself, we can go out to love even as we are loved, and hence free many from the paralysis that loneliness causes.

In Illness and Death

The last potentially inimical dimension of our lives that can limit appreciation of our own lovableness, and correspondingly make it difficult to love others, is that of illness and death. Yet, as in the other inimical forces that I have mentioned, illness and death do not have to be perceived as such if we have been leading lives of solitude and prayer. For the perspective of those who have known God's love is quite different from that of those who have seldom or never entertained the possibility that they are loved by the One who gifted them with life in the first instance.

Illness and death are not good things. As much as one may rationalize their inevitability, and stoically note that "we are born to die," death and the illnesses that herald it are never welcome. Trying to philosophize about the value of suffering is likewise futile, especially for the sufferer. Pain and the debilitating effects of physical illness can make us less human, and losing control of our bodily functions is a frightening and quite demoralizing thing. In this state we may feel far from being lovable, let alone feel like loving, and prayer is farthest from our minds. Even though our relatives and friends are supportive and are as loving as they can be, we may have difficulty receiving and savoring their love, and the psychic strength their love wants to provide is lost in the pain of the moment.

Yet I must admit that I have rarely if ever met a person of prayer who has had much difficulty accepting illness and death. This is not to say, of course, that they have been "angels" accepting the pain with equanimity, but rather that their attitude to it, their acceptance of it, pointed to a view of life that transcended their present anguish and looked beyond, at a vision of reality that did not end with death, but, in a way, became ever more vivid and real at that very point. "We die as we live," the old adage says, and those who have lived with their eyes fixed on God's great love for them die in the same way. Their cries of anguish are hence muted by a deep-down experienced conviction that all things will be well no matter the present pain-filled process of debilitation. This they know, for they have known the extent of God's love for them in all the events and foibles of their lives. Their conviction is based not on an intellectual assertion of faith in a good and loving God alone, but on past experiences of his love in a life led in close companionship with him.

However, many of us have not attained this level of sanctity. Even though we may have prayed throughout our lives in one way or another, our experiences of God have not been sufficiently profound to support us when confronted with illness or death. It seems that when we find ourselves in these situations we often feel helpless and awkward, not quite knowing how to act or what to say. As much as we may want to be kind and loving, negative feelings may result. Dealing with them in a constructive way can enable healing and love to return.

Let me try to describe some difficulties one may have in loving at a time like this, and also try to deal with the process of enabling love to bud if we are the one trying to help. There are many negative emotions that one may feel when ill, but two of them are fairly common. They are guilt and anger.

Guilt is one of those inimical forces that appears to be on a rampage in today's world. It appears, sometimes in acute form, when one is ill. It can cripple love and complicate the healing rather than remedy it. Guilt is a type of anxiety and is actually a form of fear. It is based on a spurious feeling of having violated one's own standards of love or responsibility. The unspoken belief can go something like this: "If I had taken better care of my health, and had listened to my wife's advice instead of brushing it off so easily, I would not be so sick right now." Or, "If I had been more controlled in my drinking and had gone home instead of stopping off at that bar I would not have gotten into this accident in the first place." Guilt is a form of punishing oneself for not being loving enough. Whether, in fact, one had been more than loving enough is beside the point. Guilt operates out of a fear of losing one's own self-respect, for in guilt is contained the sense of having let oneself down. It is inward looking, and the inherent punishment it brings is a way of assuaging the remorse or the sting of conscience that accompanies it, for punishment relieves guilt and reduces its torment, even though this is most often only a temporary relief. Usually guilt deals with unrealistic beliefs and is an exaggeration

126

of one's responsibilities in a given situation, though it could also be a very realistic feeling. However, at times of illness or death it is very hard to differentiate them. What can one do in a situation like this? It is important, no matter the reluctance, to force oneself to pray, to take the guilty feelings (be they realistic or unrealistic) and admit them to a loving Father God and express them to him. It is important not to hold them in but voice them, believing, though not necessarily feeling, that the God-within is very present to one's cries. In the process of expressing one's guilt, healing can begin, for the very act of praying here is an act of faith in God's loving forgiveness. The more one prays the more one can feel his forgiving love, and in that begin to forgive oneself and return to an appreciation and love of oneself again. It is very important, I repeat, to force oneself, initially, to pray even though the feelings of unworthiness will fight against that. Cry out to God for mercy and he will soon bring the perspective one needs to return to a more balanced view of things. Then the healing can begin; the love can again become evident.

But prayer alone is not enough. To facilitate the healing process in the assuaging of the guilt it would be most helpful to have someone to talk to. If one is in the hospital one could ask for the hospital chaplain, or talk to one's own minister or even a close friend who empathizes with one's condition. Love can once again enter one's life if one engages in this twofold process of expressing one's guilt to God and to a friend.

How does the friend or minister enable the process to bring the desired healing? It seems that at times like this it is very important for one to be present in a caring way to the guilty person. This is done by allowing the person to speak out his or her remorse. It is important not to interrupt with exclamations like "But you couldn't help that" or "How could you have known all that?" or phrases like that. Listen to the person. When he or she has finished, ask simple questions directed toward clarifying matters, but also directed toward establishing a proper perspective on the subject for the guilty person. For example, the guilty one may have said, "I wish I hadn't gone out that night and stayed up so late. I'm sure my heart attack was brought on by that." In reply to this one may say, "Why, were you feeling ill when you went out?" The sick person may say, "Well, not really, but I wasn't feeling very well either." One could then ask, "Had you gone out before when you were feeling unwell?" The answer would be, "Well, yes, but I should have known this time was it." "How?" one could reply. "You really had no way of telling, did you?" This sort of conversation can help establish a truer perspective and also help separate the unrealistic feelings of guilt from the realistic ones.

I think that in a situation like this one must remind the guilty person that God is a forgiving God no matter what the failure. One needs to reassure the person of God's acceptance and forgiveness. I find that in the initial stage of this exchange what often happens is that the person says, "Yes, I believe that God forgives but I don't think I deserve to be forgiven." At this point one may ask whether he or she believes that his or her sin is too great for God's mercy, and whether the punishment he or she apparently wants is what God really wants. In this way one can hope to penetrate the bitter pain of guilt and bring healing and love back to the person.

It is very important to note here that some people's guilt is so great that only professional help will suffice. The most loving thing one can do then is urge the person, if one is not that professional, in as gentle and caring a way as possible, to seek that help, even offering to go with the person for the initial visit.

Anger is another negative emotion that one may feel when ill. It is also a frequently felt emotion at the death of a loved one. It can limit love, and even though one may have prayed throughout one's life, the loss of a loved one, especially if it is one who was not old and had had a full life, can cause angry feelings to emerge. Anger is a step up from guilt. If one can get angry, either at God for doing this to one or at someone else—the doctors, the hospital staff, the funeral director—then one is on the way toward a healing and a return of love. This is because an anger expressed brings out into the open one's inner feelings of guilt and fear. Often this anger can be toward God. One may say, "How could God have let this happen to me? What have I done to deserve this? I prayed, didn't I? I did everything I was supposed to do, and look what I get for it? I think this whole prayer stuff is a pile of nonsense! When it comes right down to it God couldn't care less, let alone love me."

It is very important to be able to say this, out loud, to another if possible, but also directly to God. If one has experienced God's unconditional love in the past, or even if one has not, but believes in it, then one ought to feel absolutely free to get angry with God. It is important not to let the anger be controlled or "civilized." Give full vent to it; let God have it, saying that if he really loves you he can take this, and this, and this! It can be one of the most honest prayers that one has prayed in a while and can result in a new intimacy with God, a new sense of being loved. Then, and this is very important, ask God what he has to say to your anger. Now listen. Listen as attentively as possible to the answer. It can be surprising.

Once I had a friend who was angry at God and at the world. I encouraged her to tell me all about it. She did. When she finished I asked her, "Well, and what do you think God has to say to you after all this?" She didn't answer, but almost immediately started sobbing. Through her tears she mumbled eventually," . . . that he loves me very much and would not hurt me as I have accused him of doing." It was the start of a process that very soon after returned her to a sense of her own lovableness and goodness.

Sometimes, of course, the anger can be very deep-seated. At times like this the most loving thing to do is to suggest to one's friend that professional help may be very beneficial and offer to be with that person as he or she seeks it.

I have tried to describe guilt and anger as two emotions that can interfere with and even oppose our desires to acknowledge and accept our own lovableness. They can make the world certainly appear inimical, and even if we have been leading lives of prayer the stress of illness or death of a loved one can mitigate against our knowledge of a loving God. In these instances prayer alone is not enough—though one must indeed pray—but the help of a friend or, if needed, a counselor can go a long way in enabling one to regain the sense of God's loving presence in one's life.

Prayer can effect significant changes in our lives. One of the most important of these is the recognition that deep within ourselves is a voice of abiding Love that affirms us as lovable even though the circumstances we find ourselves sometimes in can make it very difficult for us to believe this. I have tried to describe three of these areas—when there is a breakup in a relationship, when we find that we are experiencing intolerable loneliness, and when one is ailing or when there is a death in the family or of a close friend.

When these occur, the love that prayer brings us can be frequently muted. As much as we may want to experience it one can feel quite unlovable and consequently feel very unloving toward others. At times like these it is most helpful to force oneself to pray, and to confide in a friend one's fears and doubts. This can elicit from within the gentle Voice of compassion and love, and return us to a sense of our lovableness again.

Conclusion

In this chapter I have tried to describe two consequences of entering into a life of prayer—freedom and love. I feel that they are at the foundation of our humanity, and allowing them to become alive in our lives can allow us to reassert our own uniqueness as daughters and sons of our Abba Father God. This is not an easy task, however, for many are the forces that work against us.

In an effort to help surface these forces I described four places out of which our un-freedoms can originate and three places out of which love can be lost. The four places that mitigate against our freedom were family life, religion, politics and government, and economics. The three places out of which love can be lost were relationships, loneliness, and illness and death.

By no means are these meant to be exhaustive. Each one of us can supplement our own places of bondage, our own sources where love can be lost. But I mentioned these so as to give you some pointers from which your prayer can begin to lead you to a new freedom, to new love.

I also noted that prayer alone is not enough. When one is in pain and is experiencing failure and death, formal prayer alone has difficulty penetrating our anguish. Fortunately, our God, in incarnating his Son Jesus, has already demonstrated to us that he lives not only in the place of solitude but very explicitly in each one of us who believes in him. Hence it is very important that we recognize his presence in each of us and benefit from this astounding truth by reaching out to help our brothers and sisters in need, and humbly acknowledge to ourselves that we need our brothers and sisters to help us when we are in need.

This is a natural consequence of God becoming human and living amongst us. The point of this book is to invite us once again to listen to ourselves, to the people in our lives, and to the events of our days, and be able to recognize in these our God. We look for God in so many places and wonder why he is not to be found while all the time he is in our midst, living quietly within us, and in the world around us. He is living in the hope that someday we will see that he is here, not out there somewhere, ready and always willing to love us into greater life. He is yearning for us to see, and be astounded at his true dwelling place deep within our own hearts, and realize in that sight our greatness. In that realization we see that no force on earth can dislodge us from our special place of love with him, for his love is enough regardless of the adversities of our times, the wilderness of our way. Then we can truly walk tall again and not be easily threatened no matter the danger, no matter the force.

I pray that we have the perseverance and the courage, the patience and the hope to invest our time regularly, if not daily, in this process of recognizing God's love for us through prayer, and through one another arrive at a vision of God and of ourselves that reveals the Beautiful Place where peace and justice dwell, where hope and love can kiss.